In Buddha's Kitchen

In Buddha's Kitchen

*Cooking, Being Cooked,
and Other Adventures
in a Meditation Center*

Kimberley Snow

S H A M B H A L A

BOSTON & LONDON

2 0 0 4

Shambhala Publications, Inc.
Horticultural Hall
300 Massachusetts Avenue
Boston, Massachusetts 02115
www.shambhala.com

9 8 7 6 5 4 3 2

Printed in the United States of America

⊗ This edition is printed on acid-free paper that meets
the American National Standards Institute z39.48 Standard.

Distributed in the United States by Random House, Inc.,
and in Canada by Random House of Canada Ltd

Interior design and composition: Greta D. Sibley & Associates

The Library of Congress Catalogues the previous edition
of this book as follows:
Snow, Kimberley
In Buddha's kitchen: cooking, being cooked, and other
adventures in a meditation center/Kimberley Snow.—1st ed.
p.   cm.
ISBN 1-59030-047-5 (hardcover)
ISBN 1-59030-147-1 (paperback)
1. Snow, Kimberley. 2. Buddhists—United States—Biography.
3. Spiritual biography—United States. 4. Cookery—Religious
aspects—Buddhism. I. Title.
BQ988.N69 A3 2003
294.3'923'092—DC21
2002152896

For recipes, artwork, photographs, more poetry from Leo, and
advice from the chef, please visit Kimberley Snow's Web site at
www.snowlight.com.

To Barry

Contents

Acknowledgments

MY THANKS TO COLEMAN BARKS for permission to use his translation of Rumi's poem "Chickpea to Cook"; to my husband, Barry Spacks, for his unstinting support and for Leo's poems; and to all the wonderfully helpful people at Shambhala Publications, especially my editor, Emily Bower, for her insight and kindness.

i

Boned, Minced, Reduced by Half

ONE

Retreat Doing?

THREE VOLUNTEER WORKERS and I were fixing lunch, standing on either side of the long prep table that dominated the room. Huge pots and frying pans hung from the wrought iron rack over the table.

"Whoever put tile floors in this kitchen should be shot," a woman named Celie complained.

"Or be made to stand on them for hours and hours." I sighed, looked around for the thick rubber "fatigue mat." Someone had taken it out back to use as a doormat. Someone was always doing something like that.

Chop, chop, chop.

We worked in silence for a few minutes, then talked about the girl from L.A. who had come in that morning to say she only ate range-free chicken and fresh melon. She hoped that wasn't going to be a problem for the kitchen.

Learning at last to watch my mouth, I hadn't said out loud that it might be a problem for her, but it wouldn't be for the kitchen. Just pretended I hadn't heard. But the more I subvocalized my negative thoughts, the darker my mood became. I remembered yesterday's teaching by Lama Longtalk—not his real name, but it came close—

about the man who placed a black stone on a pile for every negative thought he had, a white one for every positive thought. At first, he produced a mountain of black stones, a tiny heap of white ones. At the end of ten years, he had only white stones in front of him. A happy man.

How can anyone watch their thoughts for a single day, much less years and years, I wondered glumly. Am I supposed to be doing that?

The talk in the kitchen turned to the dressing for the beet and apple salad we were having for lunch. Belinda, from New Mexico, slipped the cooked beets out of their skins, then wiped her hands on a new white apron. I knew the red stains would never come out, but I didn't say a word. With another sigh, a deeper one this time, I remembered the good old days when I'd been able to fire someone on the spot, scream at them to get out of my kitchen and never, ever come back. Back in the days when I'd been able to control every aspect of kitchen life like a monarch. Back when they'd called me God.

I'd had a large staff then, especially when we hosted the horse sales and I fed around eight hundred people in one afternoon. I had to run a tight ship. I'd hire every reliable person I had ever worked with for the event. Semireliables (a much larger group) were also on call. I remembered a staff meeting we'd had the week before D day where I explained everything in detail. The bulk food would be brought in the day of the sales: the bread stored in the closet behind the bar, the rest to be taken upstairs, assembled and garnished, then carried downstairs as needed. One person would act as a gofer, nothing else, just a gofer, always available at the wink of an eye to leave and get whatever we needed. Susie in charge of tea and coffee, nothing else. Keep the coffeemaker going; use the gallon jugs of iced tea to fill the pitchers. Make sure the glasses are full of ice; get it from behind the bar. Pete to see that the buffet table stays fully stocked. When something looks like it's getting low, not when it's already gone, but before that, when it begins to wane, come upstairs and get another platter full of whatever. We'll have the backup platters all ready in the kitchen.

"Any questions?" I asked the assembled group.

A bored silence, then one hand went up. "Anybody got any speed?"

Can't say that I missed the old days, although it was nice to be able to fire people. Somehow it is easier to be God than Buddha, easier to control rather than cooperate. At least at first it seems that way.

The Tibetan Buddhist retreat center I'll call Dorje Ling occupies over two hundred acres of hills and forest dotted with buildings, statues, reflecting pools, a woodworking shop, a small canteen, and numerous cabins snuggled into the bushes. Lines and lines of colorful prayer flags hang from poles or trees behind a row of eight stupas.

When I went down to the garden to pick parsley for the soup, I saw, along with regular American people in sweats or tattered jeans, red-robed Asian monks, women with embroidered Tibetan aprons over long wraparound dresses called *chubas*. Several children ran through the grass chasing a ball. A stocky little blond boy, with a plastic machine gun in one hand and a Tibetan prayer wheel in the other, seemed to be the leader. Peacocks, in their own large cage, let out raucous screams at odd intervals. Large dogs drowsed in the sun. Hammering could be heard in the background.

A golf cart flying a red prayer flag was always parked near the side entrance of the main building, that three-story cream-colored stucco structure I'd gazed at so often in the photo on my bulletin board back in Kentucky. Dark red trim on the tall windows flared wide at the bottom, then narrowed toward the top, emphasizing the soaring aspect. The Tibetan-style roof with upturned gables was decorated with hand-painted designs of dragons and clouds.

The building—just like the Bluegrass Horse Center where I'd once been executive chef—grew more private the further up one went. The main shrine room, dining rooms, meeting room, and kitchen took up the first floor, while the monks, lamas, and important visitors lived on the second. The acting head of the retreat center, a Tibetan named Lama Tashi, lived on the third floor with all the painted dragons and clouds.

"Tibetans like noise," an older student from Denmark had told me as we washed up after lunch the first day of the retreat, "and company. If you have a dozen Danes and a dozen tables, you'll get one at each table, eating alone. If you have a dozen Tibetans, they'll all crowd together at one table."

"I somehow thought that retreats were silent." Unlike a Vipassana retreat I'd attended, this one was constant noise. In the shrine room, bells, cymbals, drums, long horns were all part of the ritual. Rather than traveling inward toward a personal still point, here the focus seemed to be on group activity.

"You won't get silence here. Hold on to your ear plugs."

I had heard all about Zen kitchens. The sense of order, focus. Everyone silent, bowing respectfully to each other, to the food, mindful of every minute detail. Zen master Dogen's idea that only senior students should be allowed to cook.

But Japanese Zen Buddhism was very different from Tibetan Vajrayana, and the kitchens of the two differed in the extreme. Forget the bowing, the silence, the respect. Add color, noise, and chaos. Add a kitchen full of people—construction workers looking for a snack, children playing hide and seek in the pantry, visitors using the only phone on the first floor, monks making statues out of butter and oatmeal, senior students melting coconut oil for butter lamps—fit these in the spaces around the kitchen workers and the food, and you've got the sort of kitchen I now worked in.

A high level of energy seemed to sweep through everything at Dorje Ling. Everyone was charged, pumped up with life force, buzzing with activity. And I was right out there in front like a racehorse stamping, pawing the ground, ready to break out of the chute and *go*.

Coordinate, I decided—after I'd ruined my chances for enlightenment by volunteering to take over the kitchen when the cook's back went out—*coordinate* was the operative word. I didn't have to actually cook for everyone myself—or so they said—just oversee the food. When I started asking around for an assistant, someone pointed me toward a senior student named Lonny who had once been in charge of the kitchen. But when asked if she could help out, Lonny said, "Sorry. I burn everything."

"Oh, I heard that you'd been the main chef a few years ago."

"That's true. Then I was the only cook for twelve people doing a three-year retreat. Seven men over in the right wing of the building and five women in the left. The kitchen in the middle. Literally and figuratively."

"What happened?"

"For the first few months, everyone was really into the practice, glad to be on retreat, grateful that I was supporting them by cooking. By the third year, everything had changed. People had nowhere else to go, so they'd come into the kitchen to freak out, go crazy. By then I was the main moving target of everyone's projections, hopes, and fears.

"The men would ask me to pass on messages to the women. And, of course, vice versa. Early the second year, the women took in a pregnant stray cat, and things just got worse and worse as time went on. The building was crawling with all of these felines, and some of the men found that the pussy cats were upsetting their minds."

"Nothing subtle about *that*."

"Right. So we had the whole male/female thing, and the cat thing, and then some of the retreatants would become obsessed with the person next to them or across the way, so they'd come into the kitchen where I'd be chopping and talk to me endlessly about this person. Then the other person would come in and do the same. Such venom. At first I'd tried to keep the peace, to mediate, but finally I learned to be very quiet and just try to generate compassion and love for them."

"Did it work?"

"Well, it sure helped me."

"Who did the grocery shopping?"

"Some of the bulk stuff would be delivered, but mainly I went into town every few days. I finally stopped personal shopping for the group except once every two weeks. Made them write out a list and I'd only get a few items for each person. Frightening how fascistic I became, but being the only one shopping for twelve people can get pretty hairy.

"Then, with the food, they'd become obsessed by tiny little things. Oatmeal, for instance. People could fixate on oatmeal for hours, days, weeks. It didn't matter if they liked it or didn't like it, if they wanted me to serve it with raisins and sunflower seeds or with salt and butter. They'd develop this sort of oatmeal tunnel vision. William James said, 'Whatever you attend to becomes your reality.'"

"So these people on the three-year retreat . . . ?" I didn't quite know how to formulate the question. Lonny didn't help. "So the three-year retreat isn't always, um, successful?"

"With some it is, yes, incredibly so. Look at Lama P. He was on that retreat. With others, no. It was a disaster. Partly it depended on their motivation for going into retreat in the first place."

"Motivation?" I had noticed how often this word came up at Dorje Ling.

"If they were hiding from their sexuality or their psychological quirks, then there would be problems. Or if they were motivated by their image of themselves as a spiritual person, they didn't get very far."

"But aren't the ones who choose to go into a long retreat the pick of the crop, so to speak?"

"Not necessarily. Some pretty serious students don't do group retreats. They tend to be quiet about their practice."

Later I found out that Lonny had done years of retreat herself, but never mentioned the fact. Sitting next to her was like nestling down beside a boulder. Solid, stable, nonjudgmental. Yet there was something soft about her, too, something almost flowerlike in her face. An open sweetness, even tenderness, but without sentimentality. Just clarity.

"Do you really burn everything?"

Lonny didn't answer, just looked through my eyes into something deep within me even while drawing me into her heart. This exchange was so sudden that I couldn't have resisted even if I'd wanted to. When Lonny left, I found that I had tears in my eyes.

Over and over I discovered that the senior students—and I could identify them by the fact that they seldom talked about themselves, but always listened attentively—had a certain quality, a certain presence that I had never encountered anywhere else.

From now on, I decided, much too late, I'm going to burn everything and earn the right to sit and meditate. Even as I said this to myself, I knew that my thinking was missing something essential, though I couldn't quite put my finger on it.

The idea of a food fair comes to me during the middle of the morning meditation. I hardly notice the pain in my knees that day as I contemplate a variety of booths: a salad bar, a soup station, potatoes with toppings, rice with . . . But maybe we shouldn't have rice and potatoes the same day, better on alternate days. When the lunch bell sounds, I'm surprised at how short the session has been.

As always, we end by dedicating the merit generated by our practice to the welfare of all sentient beings, and I realize that I've hardly done any real practice. But doesn't helping to feed real people count? And who's doing the counting?

In Tibetan Buddhism, different types of energy are represented by what are called the five buddha families, and each of the five is associated with a color, among many other qualities. Gold or yellow, for instance, symbolizes the Ratna family's involvement with wealth, enrichment, and generosity. In one of the many ceremonies at Dorje Ling, a specially marked tray is passed around and each person throws a flower onto it. Where the flower lands on the tray indicates the particular buddha family with which the individual has the strongest connection. My flower always fell to the north, on the green area of the Karma family, the one involved in activity. In fact, the person representing this family is usually shown in profile since she doesn't have the time to turn around fully to face you. No matter how hard I try to make my flower hit somewhere else on the tray, it always, always lands on the Karma buddha family.

During the afternoon session, I develop the idea of food booths in more detail. Soups, salads, breads blossom into Soups & Stews, Salads & Fruit, Breads & Sweets. During lunch, I'd found some large plastic bins that fit into even larger tubs that I could pack with ice and use for the salad bar. A trip to the shop reveals cans of spray paint to use on some rusty metal shelves that I'd unearthed. My hope of relaxing into emptiness recedes with each detail, each list.

Fortunately, I've brought my laptop, so at the break, I go back to my cabin and start converting recipes to feed a large group. I've just worked out a few step-by-step work lists when I hear the dinner gong. I'd forgotten to go back after the break! Maybe tomorrow, I tell myself (my face in profile, working away), I can return to sitting.

That night, I don't go into the shrine room at all but into the kitchen, empty and quiet at last. I settle in the storeroom, checking supplies and making lists. More than anything, I want to serve simple, wholesome food that doesn't distract from everyone's retreat, and to create a workable system that gives me time away from the kitchen. I'd forgotten just how much I enjoyed the administrative part of being a chef. The more planning I could do, the better.

"What doing?" Lama Tashi catches me by surprise as I'm sitting on the floor of the pantry surrounded by my laptop and portable printer, by written-over lists and schedules, books, banners of material that say POTATOES and SALADS and such. Born and raised in Tibet, Lama Tashi has a funny way of speaking English that the students both imitate and use as pith instructions. "What doing, do!" is a favorite kitchen slogan to shout at distracted helpers. "Why so much attachment having?" is taped up near the prep table.

"Meditating not?" he asks. I shake my head and try to get up, but he motions for me not to. The laptop is indeed on top of my lap. He just stands there, interested, present. I tell him that I am planning the food for the retreat.

"In Tibet. One pot. Big spoon." He picks up a plastic pail from the corner and mimes dishing out spoonfuls of food to waiting bowls. Does he really expect me to use a pail and a big spoon?

"Lama Tashi, I used to be a professional chef," it comes in a rush, "and I thought that if I just planned enough we could have sort of like a food fair with different booths. One for salads, one for soups, another station for sandwiches, and so on." I'd actually planned to have the shop make small booths and the sewing group run up signs in the colors of the buddha families and string prayer flags between, but I suddenly see all this as the sheerest folly, excessively elaborate in a way that only southern women can manage. Lama Tashi doesn't say a word, just stands there in silence as the contents of my mind open to me in a new and not very flattering light. My plans are not exactly pointless or silly, but I'm so invested in my concept of a dazzling, original food fair that I can barely think of anything else. Not for the last time in the presence of a Tibetan lama, I feel as if I am operating on several planes at once, one of which allows me to see the full extent of my grasping and ignorance. My attachment is truly staggering. But I take it in without guilt or recrimination, simply with unprecedented clarity. Simultaneously, I can also see that my motivation is good, that I do want to help.

"You good worker," Lama Tashi says, nodding approvingly. "But you *so* busy being you!" He flashes a big smile and is gone.

TWO

Religious Roots

"EXAMINE YOUR RELIGIOUS ROOTS," the teacher in the front tells the group in the meditation hall. She wears a dark red robe with her brown hair piled on top of her head, pierced by a chopstick. "Pay homage to what you've found valuable."

It felt marvelously real back then just to sit there despite the stacks of ungraded midterm exams waiting for me at home. So few people I knew at the university could even use the word *religious* without embarrassment. So rational, all my friends and colleagues in those days.

"What has provided feelings of unity and connection in your life?" the teacher continues. "Think about the source of mystery, of spirit. Try to be positive and pay tribute where tribute is due. From time to time, especially if you're stuck or feel you need to get back on track, go to your breathing. Breathe in. Breathe out. That's all you have to do. Let everything go. Thoughts will arise. That's their job. Let them alone. Just pay attention to your in-breath and out-breath. If you like, count *one* as you breathe in and again *one* as you breathe out. Then count *two*, in, out. Do this until you reach five, then start with one again. Let the mind settle in this way. When your mind is relaxed and open, return to contemplating your religious roots, paying respect, giving thanks."

Big Presbyterians, they said of my family in South Carolina. Elders in the church, taught Sunday school, hosted visiting missionaries, filled the church with flowers. Big Presbyterians. Had the minister and his wife to Sunday dinner.

I would spend the Sunday service trying not to hear the dry drone of the preacher's voice. Count the organ pipes, study Becky Taylor's new outfit, examine the stained-glass picture of the Last Supper, daydream. Couldn't remember once connecting with anything said from the pulpit. My father, sitting beside me, would note in his small neat hand how much time it took for the opening prayer (11:02–11:04), the first hymn, the sermon, the closing prayer. After church, he'd always report to the preacher, "You prayed two minutes longer today than last Sunday," or "Right on the dot today." The point of the service was to finish, to get out so we could get on with life. Church always meant waiting, never being there.

What to pay respect to? What's of value? The women, I decided. The pies and cakes at the church suppers. Community.

Christian love's a good thing. Wish Big Presbyterians were better at it.

Breathe in. Breathe out.

Around junior high one of the deacons started giving these lectures at Sunday night youth service. Girls who let boys "take advantage" became Damaged Goods. And he wasn't even talking about Going All The Way. This was in the fifties.

"Now, when you enter a store and look up on the shelf," the gray-haired deacon in his gray suit and with his gray face said sorrowfully, "are you going to want something that's been handled, been damaged by someone else? No, indeed, you're going to pick out something fresh and new."

Already too late for me to be fresh and new, too late to walk down the aisle packaged in pure white. Damaged Goods. Probably too late ever to get anywhere near heaven. Bad, bad, bad. Pretty soon I started skipping Sunday night youth service, then church altogether.

The word *Buddhism*—that round *b* with the double *d* and that extra *h* thrown in—always had a sort of glow for me. Some sort of emotional impact far below the surface. Read a few books, collected a few statues. Big draw there.

Took a yoga class once. Mind and body at one. Great stuff. Stopped doing it. Forgot why. Briefly was an apprentice Hindu when I had an affair with a guy from Lahore—all those gods. So busy.

Taoism lasted a little longer. A whole summer. Beautiful book with nature photographs. Can't remember the title. Spent lots of time wandering in the woods, relaxing into cosmic balance and harmony. Summer ended. Teaching started. Taoism evaporated. Tried to get it back. End of Taoism story.

What, then, gave me the most insight into spirit? What roots do I pay tribute to?

Drugs.

Breathe in. Breathe out.

Lots of mystical experience there. Gone with the smoke. Bad, bad, bad. When's lunch? Don't have a watch.

Maybe if I turned my neck just a little I could see the watch on the arm of the person on the cushion next to me. Damn, can't make it out.

Mescaline showed me that my own little reality wasn't the only one going. Ecstasy once. Great sex. Acid. Like putting reality through a Cuisinart. Then all those side effects. Pot. Didn't fit with graduate school, writing articles, being serious. When did I stop taking chances? How did I get to be so gray and sober before I escaped? I became a chef to get away from those towers, only to go running back to the cool and dry world of words after a few years of heavy kitchen wetness.

The university. Search for Truth and Beauty. Sort of a religion. Certainly gave a sense of community, of meaning, especially women's studies. At least at first. Oh, those were the years. Different now. Too many generals, not enough field soldiers.

Poetry. Ah, yes. Lifeblood to the heart. Rilke, Rumi, Blake. Adrienne Rich. Take us beyond the beyond. Much to pay homage to there. Poetry definitely a mainline to spirit.

Much of literature, really. Learned more about conduct from George Eliot's novels than from those gray-faced deacons. Henry James. Just his punctuation a religious experience. Hard to explain how his precise mastery of the semicolon made me see God. Used to love to watch the students' faces when we'd unpack a paragraph from *Portrait of a Lady* in the Women's Lit class.

Breathe one. Breathe two.

How about the arm on the other side? Does it have a watch? Belongs to that woman Maria. Wonder if . . .

Only ten-thirty! Damn. Could get up and go to the bathroom. Sort of in the middle of the row here. Hard to get out. Don't really need to pee.

Now I do.

All those years before the university? What provided the religious element? Romance, of course.

Windswept hills, deserted beaches, sudden entrances, breathtaking exits. Ah, the drama. The intense emotions. The sex. The wardrobe. When hormones raged, life spun and danced.

But where are all those erections now?

I glance at the teacher sitting still as a mountain at the front of the room. Everyone else sitting likewise. At least those I can see. Maybe the wrigglers sit in the back row. My own cushion seems harder every minute. Maybe I should get one of those "tush-cush" things I saw in the gift shop. Lots of nice stuff in there . . .

Breathe in. Breathe out.

THREE

Nina, the Evil Kitchen Elf

DORJE LING, staffed mainly by volunteer workers who received food, lodging, and retreat time, also supported two wards. These were basically charity cases, usually people who were unable to function well or were not responsible enough to be volunteers but had been taken in for one reason or another.

I was not sure how Nina, a bone-thin Eastern European psychotic, and her brother Jorg arrived at Dorje Ling. In order to test everyone's patience, I assumed. The rumor was that they were "referred" by a retreat center teacher in Oregon who'd had enough of them for one lifetime. Sometimes the Tibetan lamas would send each other their very worst students that way; maybe it happened in Tibet as well, I don't know.

Jorg, a mechanic, was more than welcome. One of the lamas had a habit of going around to the local auctions and buying up whatever he thought the center could eventually use. As a result, these heaps of broken machinery dotted the grounds—everything from a backhoe to a rock crusher. Even a bad mechanic would have been welcomed, so the highly skilled Jorg seemed an answer to prayer. But he came with his little sister Nina. She'd spent ten years living on the streets in Berlin, dealing heroin, turning tricks, and who knows what else. She'd been in and out of rehab, diagnosed as schizophrenic, as manic-depressive, as sociopathic, as having multiple personalities. You name it, she'd worn the label. Now she was a ward at the center.

The kitchen staff could usually work up sympathy for all of Nina's suffering, but no one liked her personally because she was just plain mean. With her frizzy hair, wild eyes, and sudden, sharp movements, she looked a little like Frankenstein's bride and gave off a kind of electric-shock energy that permeated any room she entered. Even when I was working hard at the stove, I could always tell when Nina came into the kitchen. Partly because the energy changed to something red and jagged and partly because Nina loved to stand at the fluorescent light switch and flip it on and off, on and off, on and off until someone made her stop.

Aversion, they say, like anger and attachment, creates karma. If so, I'm probably tied to Nina for countless lifetimes because I'd never encountered anyone for whom I'd developed more aversion more quickly. And Nina enjoyed my irritation, fed on my discomfort, rattled my cage whenever possible.

Our other ward at the time, a local woman named Mathilde, suffered from a similar background of drugs and mental illness. She had a habit of taking off her clothes and walking around the grounds naked shouting antigovernment slogans, but usually, if you just gave Mathilde food or made sure she was taking her medication, she'd calm down, even help with the dishes.

But Nina wasn't so easy to handle. She enjoyed playing the evil elf of the kitchen: switching labels on the spices, turning the oven dial to 500°, putting a cupful of salt in the sugar bin, hiding the meat thermometer, the tops to the plastic bins, whatever we needed most. Then she'd blame what she'd done on someone else.

After one infuriating day when we made her leave the kitchen, she told her brother Jorg that I wasn't being nice to her, and he went to Lama Tashi.

"She crazy, you not," the Lama said to the assembled kitchen staff. The bottom line at Dorje Ling was that everyone had to get along.

"But, Lama Tashi, how can we fix lunch for sixty-five people when she's all over the kitchen getting into everything?"

"Good practice for *bardo*," he calmly proclaimed. The *bardo* after death and before another rebirth is often filled with wrathful deities, terrifying sights, loud noises. Tibetans teach that the chance for attaining enlightenment in this *bardo* state is high if you can maintain a steady mind. "Very good practice."

"What studying?" he asked us sternly in his funny English. Certainly not Buddhism, he told the kitchen staff—Buddhism developed compassion for every living being. We hung our heads. All of us had seen the entire shrine room brought to a halt while an ant or some other insect was taken outside so as not to be harmed. But ants are tiny and mind their own business, I thought bitterly, resentful at being treated like a naughty child.

He said we should thank Nina for showing us the limits of our patience. Most of us hadn't developed what he called large patience, an ease of mind that could see the world like an old man on a park bench watching children at play. At most, he said, we practiced restraint, and while that was better than anger, it still wasn't large patience. Some of us hadn't even learned restraint.

"But Lama Tashi—" I almost said that I was tired of being jacked around by that bad-news piece of Euro-trash, but stopped just in time, "I have a job to do. In a place this size I have to plan ahead, to have things organized, under control. Just yesterday I came into the kitchen to cook lasagna and she's drying her boots in the oven and won't take them out. What chef in her right mind can work under these conditions?"

Oh, I was right, I was righteous, but even as I talked I could see how many times "I" and "my" snuck into my speech, how much of my own suffering came from wanting control. Just before Lama Tashi shooed us all back to the kitchen, he turned to me disdainfully. "No compassion having."

They say that a guru is like a fire: if you stay too far away, you can't feel the warmth, but come too close and you get burned. Definitely singed. They also say that a guru is a mirror, reflecting your own habits and patterns back to you until you are able to break them. Despite my hurt feelings and outrage, I couldn't help remembering how many times I'd grandly dismissed someone with just such a preemptive remark.

Nocompassionhaving became my secret mantra, a constant rhythm in my head interrupting me whenever I was just about to launch myself. Reminding me to be fair when on the verge of correcting someone. Niggling at me when I packed aggression into a witty remark. Chasing me in my dreams. Casting a glaring light over a host of memories, urging me to review the patterns that kept me isolated in anger and judgment.

I dream I'm traveling across a familiar barren landscape. I've dreamed of this place often in recent months, walking, walking through its isolation, never arriving. This time the dream begins to change. Its sepia tones turn bluish white, the light harsh against frozen waste. For the first time I realize that the rocks that edge the dream-plain are made of ice. The mountains in the distance are glaciers, wind howling around everywhere shot with motes of snow. Then I wake inside the dream, alert that I'm still dreaming, aware of immense cold and loneliness. In the distance I hear the wrenching sound of ice breaking. As I begin to walk toward that terrible sound, I enter the dream again, losing a sense of being an awake witness. Something appears on the landscape: a ship, fitted out with an icebreaker, its giant jaws grabbing at the solidly packed white landmass, then crushing and grinding it into churning ice gravel. Lama Tashi stands at the helm bearing down on me.

Meditating Not

"I CAN DO IT," I'd said, waving my hand. "Piece of cake."

The question had come up during the morning meeting less than a week into the long retreat. The cook's back was out, her assistant had been called away by a family crisis, could anyone take charge of the kitchen? "I used to be a chef," I'd foolishly blurted. Sixty-five pairs of eyes turned to look at me; group need sucked at me like a vacuum. "No problem."

With the business of the kitchen neatly ticked off, we went on to talk about the sewing project of the day, which happened to be assembling bone aprons for the lama dancers. They ordered unstrung parts from a place back east called Maxibles & Mandibles, then recruited people to string the plastic duplicates of bones together into a sort of fishnet-design apron to be worn on top of the heavy brocade costumes of the lama dancers. I'd planned on volunteering to help string bones, but now my big mouth had landed me in the kitchen. Hadn't I had enough of feeding people? Why had I volunteered, except maybe to show off, to let everyone know that I used to be a chef?

Oh, ego, ego, I moaned, you don't serve me well, but how do I get you under control? Horrified at what I'd done, I fled back to my cabin in tears.

My first impression of Dorje Ling was a sense of space, a feeling of opening outward into something much larger than the enclosed world I normally inhabited. It seemed that several lifetimes rather than a few months had passed since I'd first heard of the place, since I'd come home from the university where the very stones seemed to project a sort of judgment, an attachment to a particular way of thinking. Feeling poleaxed and cross-eyed, I sat and stared at the Dorje Ling brochure a friend had passed on to me. Just looking at the buildings gave me a sense of skylike openness.

As I stood actually deeply breathing in the mountain air at Dorje Ling on the day of my summer arrival, my whole academic career seemed to dissolve into empty space. Not for the first time, I was struck with the idea that we don't have to wait until we physically die to start another life, to enter a new dream. Everything I'd been so intensely concerned about only days before—student papers, book orders, departmental back stabbing—had vanished. Before that, my intense involvement with the details of running a kitchen had dissipated just as readily when I'd moved to California. Having been a chef and then having returned to teaching seemed to be a sequence out of a dream I'd woken from. Stepping onto the retreat land, I felt a brief explosion of clarity. As if something pressed the CLEAR button in my poor, overworked operating system of self, emptying conflicting commands and useless stored files.

And now, after volunteering for the kitchen again, I lay rigid on my bed feeling that I'd thrown away my chances for happiness by opening my big mouth.

That afternoon, Renate, a fourth-year student, told me that during her first year, the students had done all the cooking. They'd divided up into six teams, and each day one of the teams would cook all three meals. On Sunday people would just fend for themselves or wouldn't eat at all.

"Did that work?"

"Yes and no. What happened was that it became this great cook-off, and by the end of the retreat, every team was trying to outdo the others by having the best meals. The gofer had to go into town for things like coconut milk for the curry or a special mango chutney. The retreat director freaked out because the costs were spiraling out of control, so he all but stopped shopping for anything but the basics. Then Tony, whose family owned an Italian restaurant, would have them mail him capers and sun-dried tomatoes. So someone on another team had her secretary start FedExing things her team needed. And so on."

I could see it all, vividly. Nor did any of it surprise me. "And they talked about all of this during the breaks, right?"

"You got it. And people started gaining weight because they were being fed these three gigantic meals a day and then sitting in meditation the rest of the time. We puffed up like balloons. I gained fifteen pounds myself."

"Just from the meals?"

"Actually, no. From chocolate. Someone had this idea that we needed a new tent to eat in—at the time we had some blue plastic draped over lines hung between trees—and we could pay for it through our store. We sold cards and notebooks and things, but mainly candy bars and peanuts. When you're doing nothing but sitting, going in and in and in, facing your shit all the time, you want some sort of compensation. For me, it was chocolate."

"So you'd have what, a bar or two a day?"

" 'It's for such a good cause,' I'd say to myself. 'I'll just buy two and give one away.' So I'd do that. Some days I'd give them both away. Then I started finding chocolate bars on my pillow that someone had left for me. Those you have to eat, right? It became this *thing* we'd do. All anonymous, all of us full of generosity, all of us gaining weight."

"Sounds like food sort of dominated the retreat."

"Uh-huh."

"Does this always happen? With the food, I mean."

"Sometimes it's sex. One year it was the temperature. No one could agree whether the window should be kept open or shut, how soon the fire should start in the morning, who should build it. The room was always too hot or too cold. I don't even remember the food that year. I guess we must have eaten. Anyway, in all these retreats other things are going on, too. Retreat-type things that you don't really discuss. Since we were told not to talk about our practice, we all talked about food or heat instead."

"Why were you told not to talk about the practice?"

"The blessing goes out of it."

I was to hear this again and again. If you have a good meditation, don't get up from your sit and publicly announce just how good it was. "Everybody," we'd joke, crooning it like Frank Sinatra, "has *samadhi* sometime." Visions, mystical experiences, transcendent emotions, no matter how vivid to the meditator, were all seen as temporary happenings: *nyam,* they were called in Tibetan. The same with a session when you found it hard to concentrate, difficult to remember what you were supposed to be doing. Just keep meditating. Everyone gave the same counsel: if someone asks you how your practice is going, just answer, "It's going."

At Dorje Ling, people on retreat shared rooms in a large house used as a dorm or lived further back in small cabins—converted sheds, really—that staggered up the hill. We'd be up and in the shrine room by six for morning practice, *puja,* held in Tibetan. After breakfast we'd go back to the shrine room for teachings and meditation. After lunch, a scheduled two-hour work period, then more teachings, meditation, and dinner. Finally, the evening session would stretch until around ten, when I would more or less fall into bed, thrumming with adrenaline.

Most of the people on the retreat were used to lengthy practice, but from the very first day my body rebelled against sitting in meditation for very long at a time. Within half an hour, I'd begun to squirm. After an hour, my knees hurt and my legs cramped in a serious sort of way. Then various muscles would jump while strange pains traveled through my body. On breaks, I'd take a look at the long line for the ladies' room, then go out back to pee in the woods like the men. Still hiding behind a bush, I'd jump up and down trying to relieve some of the tension that kept building up in my body. Or I'd shake myself all over, dog-fashion. These little fits helped to keep me from screaming in the shrine room, shrieking long and loud, pounding the floor, banging my head on the *puja* bench.

When I wasn't obsessed by physical discomfort, something happened to me in that shrine room. My mind expanded beyond self-involvement. I no longer had an individual consciousness but felt deeply embedded in a group experience that transcended the personal altogether. Suddenly I didn't feel lonely anymore, then realized that I hadn't even known I'd felt isolated, alienated before. The sense of separation had become so total it all but disappeared in my consciousness except as a background landscape I moved through. But as the group practiced together, I seemed part of something ancient, timeless, rooted. Something that reached a level for which I'd always felt a nameless homesickness.

At Dorje Ling, I sensed that I was not only in a different place, but in a completely different time as well. Despite an occasional glimpse of a cell phone or laptop, the atmosphere was almost medieval. In the self-contained fiefdom of Dorje Ling, I was absorbed into something settled, lasting, old. I almost expected to see a yak trundle by on its way to the barley fields.

I was not waiting for something, not remembering anything, not fighting against a deadline that seemed to be coming at me too soon. With past and future contained in the present, everything concentrated there at once, in the moment, happening.

But then I'd gotten put in charge of the kitchen. Or put myself in charge. It had been years since I'd worked as a chef and I had never, ever, not for a single nanosecond, wanted to return. Damn, I sniffled, feeling my new holiness dissolve like morning mist. Why does this keep happening to me?

I went to Lama S. with a new list of projects, mainly designed to get me out of that damnable kitchen and into somewhere sane like the office or the library. Somewhere I belonged. It seemed I was always trying to get *out* of somewhere or something that I'd leapt into.

Karma had landed me in the kitchen, I was told. Causes—created in this life or a past one—invariably lead to effects. But what did that mean, really? To think that perhaps I was an evil ruler who starved his subjects to death in a former life seemed too literal and naive an interpretation. Lama S. often warned that simple explanations were a mistake. Buddha himself had seen the intricacies of karma—along with the creation of the universe—as imponderable.

So what is it that karma does? Creates habits, for one thing. Every time I withdraw coldly from a situation, another link is forged in the chain mail of defenses. So that is how I create at least one kind of karma. I asked Lama P. about it and he said yes, that's one thing. Another is that karma from previous lives is ripening in the present moment and the way in which we react creates more (or less) karma. "Like that chocolate mousse you're working on," he said. "See how all the striations have blended into one?"

During meditation sessions, when I wasn't thinking about what we were going to have for lunch, I had started to design a web site for meditators. Over the weeks, I'd filled it out and now called it QuietSpaces.com. At the main menu, a variety of backgrounds could be chosen, but the graphics were minimal; just soothing space shows on the screen. Links would take the surfer to instructions or on to related sites.

When I'd arrived at Dorje Ling, Lama S. hadn't seemed especially surprised to see me, although she'd been the one to invite me up for a visit. She just gave me a short thought-so kind of nod. I always went to her first for advice and counsel. But today I seemed to be lecturing on hyperspace.

"When you click on Tara's name," I explained to Lama S., "you see a slide show of *thangkas,* hear her mantra, then a menu appears and you can read up on her historical significance as a female buddha in Tibet. Or go right to teachings on the text. I can hypertext various *sadhanas* used in morning *puja.*"

Lama S. just looked at me.

"It's not that hard, really. The material is all there in the library, it just needs to be entered into a database."

"Tell me about this Internet thing." Lama S. had just gotten a computer, but wasn't yet online.

So I told her what I knew. That the Namgyal monks held a ceremony in which they blessed cyberspace, saying that, like basic emptiness, it can't be seen, but things arise from it. And it can be used with good motivation or bad intention. In their ceremony, they prayed that everyone use cyberspace with good intention. I told Lama S. that you can still go to their site and hear them chanting the prayer.

"But what about the sex everywhere? That's all I've been hearing about."

"That's so sad," she commented when I explained chat rooms. "No warmth. No *chi,* just this electricity buzzing around in their heads."

She told me that she'd asked her own teacher once about teaching online but that he'd said it might not be a good thing. The words would come through, but he wasn't sure there would be any true spiritual transmission. People might just develop concepts about the teachings without any real wisdom.

"The saddest thing was that he said there was no one he could ask. All of his own teachers are dead. Besides, the whole subject is too new, too unknown. He finally told me he'd ask some of the younger Rinpoches, maybe they would know."

After a little while, she asked me about the kitchen, the problems with anger, the strain of having to work with others. But this wasn't what I wanted to talk to her about. "Now, about QuietSpaces.com," I began.

"How about," Lama S. said with a smile, "There, in the kitchen, you *become* QuietSpaces.com?"

FIVE

Insight

YEARS AND YEARS BEFORE, back in Kentucky, when I received a flyer for a week-long residential Buddhist meditation retreat, I tried to talk my friend Wendy into going with me during our spring break.

"But Wendy, you drive right by there." *There* being the Insight Meditation Retreat Center, five miles from her family's house, where her daughter was going to spend the week.

"Doesn't mean I have to go in. I drive right by the penitentiary, too."

"Come on. We can drop off Leslie, spend the week at the retreat center, pick her up again on Sunday. It'll be great. You can do some meditation, hike the trails around there. Leave if you don't like it."

"Except that I don't want to. A Saturday workshop is one thing, but a whole week? My only real vacation? I get to completely relax. Sleep in. No schedule. Talk only to grown-ups all week. Heaven."

"Come on, let's try it. You saw the flyer, it's that Vipassana retreat."

"Vipa-what?"

"Vipassana. Insight. Practice of the Theravadin Buddhism of southeastern Asia. Let me read you what the brochure says. 'Insight meditation focuses on creating mindfulness. . . .'"

"No, please."

"Okay, okay. Whatever. But listen, can you drop me off? I'll get a ride back with someone else."

"No problem."

I didn't know for sure that Wendy had signed up for the retreat until we actually got there, but I suspected something was up by the way she kept smiling to herself through the trip. She'd make a lousy spy.

Wendy and I weren't competitive so much as we always sort of egged each other on. If Wendy got into yoga, it wouldn't be long before I would be stretched out on a mat in the fish pose. That sort of thing. I had talked Wendy into coming to some of the early workshops I'd been attending, but she didn't seem interested in meditation or Buddhism, even though I thought she should be. For her own good.

At dinner—which they called tea and I found surprisingly light—I noticed Wendy glancing around the dining room. Everyone else—mainly women—seemed to be looking down at their plates, not talking. Uh-oh, I thought, what have I gotten us into?

In the main hall right after dinner, the head teacher, a woman named Leila, told us the schedule: the day would be broken up into forty-five-minute periods of sitting and walking meditation, interspersed with talks on

Dharma—the teachings of the Buddha. "And, of course," she added, "it goes without saying"—smile—"no talking for the seven days of this silent retreat."

I was afraid to turn my head to look at Wendy.

"Now, please," Leila continued, "don't go farther than the flags set up around the center. We're having a problem with rattlesnakes this year. And the woods are just full of poison oak. Also, now that the retreat boundaries are closed, you can't, of course, leave the property. If you have any questions, you can write a note to me or Donnie. All right? Now, time for lights out. Five-thirty comes pretty early in the morning, so we'll want to get lots of rest tonight."

On the way out, Wendy jabbed me in the ribs, hard. Then stamped on my toe as I shoved past. I didn't blame her, not really.

"Being ever vigilant about stopping your thoughts during sitting only develops the mind of a sniper." Donnie was giving the morning Dharma talk. "Meet these thoughts with loving-kindness for yourself. The brain is just doing its job, always looking out for you. Probably one reason we think about sex so much is that the survival instinct is strong in us. When our brain churns up thoughts of status, of getting ahead, it's just a modern version of finding an advantage in the hunt. We're the product of evolution, after all."

I felt like Donnie had been watching my sniper brain all morning. I'd been amazed at the constant stream of thoughts that I couldn't control, couldn't stop.

Wendy didn't show up all that morning, but sat slumped over her salad when I came into the dining room at lunch. As I sat down beside her, she turned aside and hunched over her bowl as if I had planned to steal it. For a minute or two, I tried to send her feelings of loving-kindness, but could almost hear them fizzle and pop as they reached her taut surfaces.

She did come to the afternoon session, and out of the corner of my eye I could see her stare in horrified disbe-lief as Leila demonstrated walking meditation for anyone who had missed the instruction that morning.

"The idea is to become mindful of your body, your sen-sations, so you let your attention rest on your feet and legs, on how they move. Lift right foot, place it on the ground, shift weight onto the heel, then the toe, lift left foot, place, shift weight onto the left foot. Lift right foot. . . ."

The area marked off by the flags didn't extend much farther than the parking lot, so there was something of a traffic jam during the walking meditation period. That morning I had found a nice shady spot behind the last cabin, but when I got there, Wendy was already stalking back and forth with her arms spread like Frankenstein's monster, making lock-kneed lurches. The minute she saw me, she rushed over. "You lied to me," she began, apparently having decided that the rule of quiet didn't extend to the two of us. "Up at five-thirty. No men under sixty and you can't even *talk* to *them*. And this walking meditation shit. We look like we're straight out of *Night of the Living Dead*!"

"I didn't know it was going to be silent, Wendy. Truly I didn't. Just give it a chance. The first three days of a retreat are always hell, really. For everybody." Donnie had told us so that morning. Somehow I couldn't stop playing the expert with Wendy.

Wendy fumed. I started walking. Lift, place, move.

"Self-righteous bitch," she muttered to my back.

"*Metta,* or loving-kindness, is accepting everything that happens as part of Dharma. Accepting is not the same as approval. If we accept everything that comes our way with loving-kindness—and don't forget that attention itself is a kind of *metta*—then we can maintain a calm, still center in the midst of whatever arises." This time Leila is speaking. She has a beautiful voice that unlocks something deep inside my heart.

"In the same spirit, I hear people say, 'Pain is a given, suffering an option.' Once we get outside of our stories, once we take them less seriously, we suffer less and less."

It's then that I notice that Wendy is leaning forward, listening intently. I am too, I suddenly realize.

Leila talks on about how we create these stories for ourselves, bit by bit, until we've constructed sort of a personalized theme park. We might have a display for Accomplishments, maybe a monument to Marriage. Most of us add a ride fueled by anger which loops over and over the same territory, repeatedly producing the same emotions. Maybe we have sideshows with selected videos of What Happened To Me As A Child. But, Leila concludes, the past is gone, it's over. We don't have to keep rewriting history. Visiting this theme park or redoing the exhibits keeps us from being aware in the present moment.

The same with ideas of the future. She asks how many find that their minds spin forward during sitting meditation. My own hand goes up, then almost everyone else's. This is normal, she explains. We have to plan, to think about the future, but in a reasonable way.

"Many times I find myself writing out this script of a possible future for myself and for others. But usually it's a screenplay that's never going to be optioned. Certainly not without rewriting." Leila is silent for a moment, then continues.

"We often have a sense of a gigantic past behind us, with the future as a great mass in front that needs to be muscled and pummeled into shape. And the present as this tiny crack between. But this little sliver we think of as the present is the whole thing; it's all we have. That's why we try to slow down and become mindful.

"While you're here on retreat, simply watch how many times your mind goes away from the present. Don't berate yourself for thinking of the past or the future, simply name it. Say to yourself, 'remembering' or 'planning.' Or even just label it 'thinking,' then go back to the breathing. Just follow your breath. That's all you have to do here on retreat. Sit. Breathe."

In addition to labeling my own stream of thoughts as REMEMBERING and PLANNING, I added a new category, WENDY. This included a whole range of reactions: watching, worrying, responding with regret, irritation, disappointment, love, hope, attachment, control.

Late in the week, I headed off into the woods after lunch, walking right past all of the little red flags. I needed to get away from the group to clear my head, settle my mind. Everything looked crisp, startlingly beautiful.

I was just thinking that retreat and silence were things I want more of in my life when suddenly I came upon Wendy sitting under a tree, smoking a joint. She looked relaxed, even blissful.

I rustled the leaves until Wendy's gaze drifted around to my direction.

"You were right to drag me here." She smiled in such an open-hearted way that it made me want to cry. I realized how much I'd missed being Wendy's friend all week. "I'm just beginning to understand how my stories hem me in, make me unable to take in information about other people. Especially Leslie. She's just trying to grow up." Wendy talked on about the various insights she'd experienced over the week, the deepening of understanding. "I'm so glad I came."

When she held out the joint, I shook my head. We'd both taken the five basic precepts for the duration of the retreat, vowing not to kill, lie, steal, indulge in sexual misconduct, or use alcohol or other substances.

"Oh, they didn't mean this," Wendy scoffed. "Or they don't mean us."

"I don't know. Could be some sort of karma involved here."

"Do you think?"

"Maybe there's more to all of this stuff than we can see from the Western perspective. I really don't know."

"What do you mean?"

"Well, for one thing, Wendy, right now you're sitting in a big patch of poison oak."

SIX

Shhhh

IT'S BEEN TWO WEEKS since I took a vow of silence, and as far as I can tell, no one has noticed. When people come into the kitchen here at Dorje Ling, I simply nod as they talk, sometimes murmuring "um," that neutral little sound that expresses so much and reveals so little. I can sense my reputation as a good conversationalist increasing daily.

When I first went silent, I kept fingering a pad and pen in my pocket, planning to write SILENCE, or maybe SILENT VOW, but I've never had to bother.

Today I stand by the big Hobart mixer, dumping in flour and salt, listening to its steady drone, hearing it for the first time as a sculpture of sound rather than an irritating noise one must talk over. The slosh-slosh of the dishwasher, the hiss of the burners, the controlled clamor of the fan in the hood of the stove—all have become my allies in a world without speech.

I remember the long Sunday afternoons in South Carolina when I would hide under the giant ferns and listen to the streams of talk from aunts and grandparents, all mingling into a living river of familiar voices. It seemed normal to me that the same tales, with the same digression about who was kin to whom, would be told over and over. I took it for granted that when a gap opened, someone had to rush in to fill it up with words, sounds, stories. As I listen to the steady drone of the kitchen machinery, my body relaxing into mechanical rhythms, I feel no urge to add my voice to the clamor of the world. I've come to see most talk as a sort of verbal littering that blights and obscures the vastness of the landscape. When talk is happening, other things don't happen, can't. These other things are what I am after.

And I'm not about to start talking again until the silence has done its work. Even then, it will take something truly substantial to make me speak.

I am a happy woman now although that has not always been the case. At times in my life, in fact, I've been downright miserable.

Years before this vow of silence, my misery had been deep and dense, hardening and dark around me like the crust on an over-fried turnover. My latest marriage had failed, and my new career, that of a chef, wasn't working out.

Oh, I'd been successful in food service; that wasn't the problem. In fact, I'd worked up to something of a dream job as executive chef of a private club at a center where racehorses were trained and sold. I could order pounds and pounds of crabmeat, fresh raspberries out of season, the rarest spices and chutneys. The butcher automatically saved me the best cuts, the prime meats. The fish vendor fell all over himself to get me exactly what I wanted. I had only to pick up the phone and he'd bring it out. Sometimes he'd even call me: "Live lobsters. Flown in this morning. How many would you like?"

And I had big shiny pots to cook the lobsters in, utensils to crack the shells, pretty little bowls for the drawn butter. My kitchen shelves groaned under the weight of tools and appliances: espresso machines, pasta makers, even my own electric sesame seed grinder. Then there were smaller kitchen gadgets by the boxful: chocolate shavers, butter curlers, parsley mills.

No one ever took me to task for spending. I kept books, but no one ever went over them to point out that this was extravagant or how I could save money if I did—or didn't do—this or that. No one even hinted that I should cut down or economize. So why worry?

Nor did I have to wash a single dish or clean so much as a tiny spill on the stove. The staff, beaten at last into submission, left me alone, did their jobs, didn't talk back. Among themselves, they referred to me simply as God. "I don't know," they'd say without rancor. "I'll go ask God."

Workers at the large complex that housed the club smiled and asked what was for lunch, busy in their own worlds of training and selling racehorses. Local papers and magazines ran stories on the center, took pictures of me in my chef's hat, smiling and smiling. The owner of the Bluegrass Horse Center continued to beam benignly and call me "the best damn chef in the world."

And what did I want?

I wanted out.

I wanted never to have to think about food again, never to plan a meal, never to order groceries, never to touch an egg or a frying pan, never to . . . well, you get the idea.

Even as I continued to boil down the *fumé* or work butter into the puff pastry, I began to have little fits. Suddenly, I'd find myself stir-frying bits of quiche with hunks of chocolate cake. Would slam these into a mold, knead a little heap of fresh garbage into it, make a well in the center and fill it with dark, wet coffee grounds. Then I'd top it off with an exquisitely decorated petit four and perhaps a dab of whipped cream. I would let this pile sit, casting quick glances toward it while I cooked. Then, sometime after lunch, I'd smash an egg onto its very top, smearing the pink rose frosting into the coffee grounds, into the pâté. If the egg didn't happen to break, I'd pause again, and watch it, pleased, waiting. I'd take a silver knife from the dining room, toss it from hand to hand in front of the dish or sometimes draw the back of it gently over the egg. As I planned the next day's menu, I'd spin suddenly and crack the egg with precise violence, fragmenting its pure white shell, breaking its wholeness. Smiling, I'd watch the albumen drip out little by little and ooze down over the mountain of broken forms, of smashed rules.

Sometimes poor burnt-out me would take everything from the refrigerator, all of the little dits and dots of things saved but never used. Take them all out and pour them onto a single platter, kneading them together until I felt better. Once, when a cup happened to break, I garnished the platter with its shards.

If anyone happened to come into the kitchen during one of these little fits, they left quickly, throwing frightened glances over their shoulders. People began to avoid me. I knew, but I didn't care. On my time off, I would cook things that combined French and Indian ingredients with Chinese techniques, unnameable messes. For lunch, my own lunch, I'd slop together foods that had no history, no method, maybe salsa on pound cake. I would seek out things to eat that tasted bad, looked horrid. I found it unbearable to sit down to a normal meal. Standing at the counter in my tall chef's hat, I started to eat out of tin cans and jars, off the back of pie plates.

The more I came to hate the goddamn perfection of the food I prepared each day and resent the compliments it received, the more exhausted I felt. A certain type of exhaustion never left me, the kind of tiredness that comes when you are not being refueled, when your work doesn't feed your soul.

I'd look out into the dining room at the soft good old boys and their beautiful, manipulative women: all waiting for food, waiting to be pleased, to be served, serviced. "Go out and gather nuts and berries," I'd mutter inwardly to the spoiled and greedy. "Eat gruel." Then the poor hapless waiter would come in with his orders, push the tickets at me, and flee to the safety of the pantry.

"It all turns to shit," I'd think as I sent out dish after dish of beautifully textured Roquefort mousse, creamy scallion soup with an undercurrent of good white wine, delicately flavored coquilles St. Jacques, luscious white truffles garnished with sprigs of fresh mint. "Nothing but shit."

I escaped, finally, to a teaching job in California, although I'd said I never wanted to see the inside of a classroom again. At first, it seemed like a dream to never carry anything heavier than a book bag, to be able to come home without olive oil spatters on my clothes. I especially liked the fact that no one in the department raced horses. I let myself again be embraced by the cool, dry world of words. Little Kimberley, happy at last.

But soon I'd reached the same level of burnout, of dissatisfaction with my job, my students, with teaching itself as a profession. I'd begun to attend weekend retreats and workshops to at least begin to understand this inner void. Southern California provides a smorgasbord of gurus, teachers, swamis. Without even leaving town I could take seminars on rebirthing, shamanic journey, Sufi dancing almost every weekend. With my friend Wendy, who also taught women's studies, I went to a series of Saturday workshops on the different spiritual paths and began to meet Buddhist teachers.

"This retreat time has been so incredible," I told Lama S. on the last day of a Tibetan Buddhist retreat in Ojai. "I feel like I've gone into another dimension."

In the other weekend workshops I'd attended, I'd felt interested, challenged, entertained. I'd sometimes experience short-lived bliss or a sense of unity and clarity. But when I met Lama S. and the Tibetan meditation master she translated for, I experienced a shift in my consciousness, entered a space I never even knew existed. During the last chanting, I started crying and hadn't been able to stop.

Lama S., originally from Idaho, had recently com-
pleted a three-year retreat in Nepal. Her beauty started
somewhere deep in her bones and became more radiant
as it neared the surface. When I sat next to her, I never
wanted to be anywhere else, just there.

"Have you done other retreats before?" she asked.

I gave Lama S. a rundown of the various events I'd
attended.

"Well, it's important for you to see what's out there,
what you respond to. But at a certain point it's a little like
drilling for oil, you know. You can't just dig a few feet
here, a few feet there. You have to keep going down, down
in one spot."

I knew that I was more the butterfly type, flitting
from thing to thing. Always leaving, never staying to
work it out.

"Do you have a daily practice?"

"Well, not actually." I wasn't even sure what Lama S.
meant. "I'm going to start writing again every day. I decided that this morning."

"Writing?"

"Well, I'm thinking about a lot of different possibilities." I sketched my list of potential projects, which included a novel about Buddha's aunt, who'd raised him, a
vegetarian cookbook, and a web site for meditators. All
of these had come into my busy mind during the morning meditation.

Lama S. listened carefully, intently. When I'd finished, she sat a bit straighter, flipped a few beads on her
mala, looked at me in front of her, sighed, went back to
her *mala.* Finally she said, "You know, all these projects,

you're just rearranging the clouds. What you really need is to concentrate on the nature of sky. I think you should do a serious retreat."

As Lama S. spoke, I experienced the sense of space I'd felt on the first meditation session with her. Without quite knowing it, I'd been hoping, straining to catch another hint of this openness ever since. But sky had been there all along, waiting for me to stop hoping and straining, to quit pushing the clouds around.

When Lama S. left, she'd given me a little clay statue called a *tsa-tsa* and some information about the retreat center where she lived in northern California. The cover photo of the retreat center's brochure showed a large Tibetan-style building ringed by open fields with a row of *stupas* off to the left. Colored flags were strung on the trees on either side of the building and blue mountains rose in the distance. Timeless, peaceful.

I couldn't forget the way I'd started crying during the Tibetan chanting at the end of the retreat with Lama S. Its beautiful ancient melody opened a secret door deep inside. I felt a tug there, the faint stirring of new life coming into being.

The little *tsa-tsa* gift rested on the top of my desk, and I'd hung the picture of Dorje Ling on my bulletin board above it. In time I developed the habit of sitting and looking at the picture when I came home from school, imagining myself in that open space, walking up to that big yellow building. Every day, I took something else off the board—an invitation to an art opening I'd decided not to attend, the times for a movie that no longer

seemed interesting, a flyer for a lecture I'd never hear—
so that the area around the photo became more and
more empty. When the picture was the only thing left on
the board, I decided to attend a month-long retreat at
Dorje Ling.

SEVEN

Living Dharma

I HAD PLANNED to leave right after the retreat, but I didn't. Somehow I couldn't make myself go. Besides, there was no one to cook lunch. Then dinner. Then breakfast. Then I got a call from the people who'd sublet my house. They wanted to stay on through the summer. Since I didn't teach again until the fall, it all worked out for me to stay at Dorje Ling for another few months. When Diane, the head chef, finally came back, at last I had a chance to catch my breath and settle into the place.

About thirty people made up the population of Dorje Ling. Each person had his or her own room or cabin. Some of the senior students had built houses in the hills that ringed the center, one a beautiful cedar house made from a kit. Some of the places had elaborate gardens with waterfalls, reflecting pools, and statues—the sort of landscaping that takes infinite patience. Other houses nestled in the woods so inconspicuously that it seemed they had grown there, not been built by the people who lived in them.

Most of the staff were interested not just in building but in creating new forms, unusual habitats. One couple lived in a place with walls constructed from packed mud, another in a geodesic dome. Near the top of a hill, a straw-bale retreat house was under construction. Several people lived in big round Tibetan tents, yurts. The construction crew sat enchanted all through lunch one day when a visiting contractor from Minnesota described a house that looked like a beehive, made from long tubes filled with sand, wound round and round. I figured it was only a matter of time before someone started one on the center's land.

Next to building, people at Dorje Ling—including the lamas—liked to sew. Using long metal shears, the Tibetans would cut into silk brocade to create what seemed to be the strangest sorts of shapes. They never used a pattern, didn't even seem to be paying much attention to what they were cutting, but then they'd sit at the sewing machine and stitch together perfect costumes for the lama dancers, or a *chuba* for one of the women or a new jacket for a friend.

Once when we were in the sewing room, trying on the long-sleeved Tibetan blouses that go under the *chubas,* Madeline said, "When's the last time you had a breast exam?"

Madeline, one of the staff, was a nurse practitioner in town, also a midwife.

"Who are you talking to?"

"Everybody. All of you." There were only women in the room that day. "Listen up. This is important. When's the last time you had a breast exam?"

"Maybe two years ago," Diane admitted.

"Take off that blouse." Madeline did a quick exam, first on Diane, then the rest of us. "Okay, now all of you examine yourselves every month. Like this." She showed us all how, using Diane's exposed breast. We heard footsteps and managed to close the door before the monks passing by the sewing room looked in and saw a room full of jiggling boobs. The situation sent us all into such gales of laughter that Diane wet her pants.

That day was the first time we practiced the Laughing Lotus Sutra. We'd meet, start laughing, laugh until we wept. Some would start crying right away; others would pretend they weren't, simply wipe away tears that could be from crying or from laughter or from both. That was the state we all aimed at, that clear light of simply feeling what we were feeling without resistance, without going off on mental trips about it. Just feeling, openly, peeling back our chest walls to the exposed heart. Some pounded their chests, hoping to break up the encrustation there, to relax the tension of living together, of putting on an event, of simply being human. To some of us women who worked in various corners of Dorje Ling, the office or the store or the publishing arm, the Laughing Lotus Sutra came to be almost a daily practice.

Certain things were hard to explain to the Tibetan monks. Daylight saving time, for instance. Personal space. Birthday parties. Psychiatry. They'd listen politely, shrug, and go on their cheerful way. The Westerners had trouble understanding things as well. Emptiness, for instance. I heard Lama Tashi describe it this way: "Emptiness nothing not. Emptiness something not. Always arising display. Emptiness something nothing beyond."

For an instant, briefly, just when he was talking to me, I understood emptiness completely. But when I'd try to get an intellectual grasp on it, I rarely could, especially at first.

During events, people would drive up from the Bay Area, fly in from Boston, Hawaii, come out of the nearby woodwork. Since I worked in the kitchen, usually I'd only meet the people who signed up for food prep shifts or those who came in to ask for something special like fresh papaya juice. They'd add, "I hope that won't be a problem," a phrase that I found people in California tended to use instead of "please."

A number had health problems or were food faddists of some sort or another. Diane always surprised me by being patient and compassionate with retreatants who'd come in to boil pots of herbs when we were cooking dinner for over a hundred. I would have thrown them out on their ear, but Diane had a different way of being in the kitchen, one that had to do with something other than control. Everyone at Dorje Ling tried to live out the teachings, to put them into action. Not once but every minute of their lives.

The senior students were a constant amazement to me. They weren't goody-goody saints, but very smart, very focused human beings. Yet they didn't lose their tempers, didn't get impatient with the rest of the group, not even with the visitors who were sometimes unspeakably rude and arrogant. The senior students just continued to be steady and compassionate.

"Please," I would pray when I lost my temper yet again, "let me be like them."

But Lama S. told me that it was all a trickle-down effect. She said that she always prayed to be like her teacher, the one who now lived in Nepal. Whenever the senior students talked about him, they'd get this look in their eyes: reverence, admiration, gratitude, and awe all mixed together. Whoever he was, his effect on them was profound: they were the most selfless and compassionate humans I'd ever encountered.

At that time, I felt that I hadn't really met my own teacher yet, hadn't found the Rinpoche (the Tibetan honorific title for a revered teacher) who would help me on a personal level. In the meantime—and I was a newcomer to all of this—the teachings of the holy Dharma flowed into my mindstream like water into a parched garden.

Practice went on night and day at Dorje Ling. Before I'd moved there, I thought that I would spend lots of time in silent meditation, but it rarely happened. Instead, daily conduct—compassionate interaction, mindfulness— was the point. During morning and evening *puja,* we would chant a text, or *sadhana,* together in Tibetan, visualizing the various deities as we went along. Concentrating on each syllable developed a sort of one-pointed concentration. Envisioning the qualities of each deity allowed us to experience the potential of that quality in ourselves—at least that was the idea. I found it difficult to visualize and remained completely hopeless when it came to chanting. The Tibetan sounds fell apart in my southern mouth, a hopeless mash and mess. I often re-sorted to saying "pasta primavera, pasta primavera" over and over so that at least my lips were moving.

Maybe I could blame it on being raised Presbyterian, but I'd never really known how to respond to rituals. Every now and then I could forget myself, override the imprints of Knox and Calvin in my very brainpan, and feel a connection with chanting, with incense, with the complicated activities of the shrine room, but not often. The former Catholics in the group could just dive in and enjoy themselves, but I sat stiff and uncomfortable, glad when *puja* was over.

The teachings, on the other hand, were like pure gold. I'd never been told how my mind worked, never been in-structed in ways to control it or even told that it should be controlled. No one had ever mentioned karma to me or explained the poisons of the mind, much less ways to lessen their damage. Or let me in on the secret that spon-taneous compassion begins to flow into the places va-cated by the poisons. All my life I'd felt that I'd been missing an owner's manual or rather had been given the wrong one. Now, suddenly, the little gaps were being filled in and glitches getting worked out. I would have willingly endured hours of *puja* to get to those teachings. In fact, I often did.

"I just don't see how you can go off and live with all those heathens," my mother said on the phone after I had been at Dorje Ling for a few months. I'd made the mistake of telling her about a Rinpoche who was visiting from Bhutan.

Every phone call, the first thing my mother asked was when I'd be leaving. No explanations seemed possible.

"You can't just remove yourself from life like that."

"Mother . . ."

"And don't start telling me about that Ricochet of yours . . ."

"*Rinpoche,* Mother . . ."

I complained to Lama P., "My mother keeps saying how selfish I am." It really bothered me that my family accused me of being self-centered just at the point when I'd been working so hard to start moving in the opposite direction. "Mother sees meditation as something that makes people detached and cold."

"How old is she?"

"Eighty-something."

He shook his head. "Wouldn't expect her to change much now. The way you act around her might eventually influence her, but it really doesn't matter what she thinks. She's wrong, so big deal. Let her be wrong."

I had never thought of it that way at all. Couldn't even come up with a reply.

"Compassion works in all sorts of ways, you know. Sometimes it's just pulling back and being quiet. Sometimes it means challenging someone. Usually not. Atisha says . . . Do you know Atisha?"

"He's the slogan guy?"

"Yep. Eleventh century. His *Seven-Point Mind Training* has a list of slogans to work with. One of his sayings is 'Don't bring things to a painful point.' I think that might apply to the situation with your mother."

"Tell me some others."

"Well, there's 'Be grateful to everyone.' 'Don't wait in ambush.' 'Don't seek others' pain as the limbs of your own happiness.' My favorite is 'Always apply a joyful mind.'"

"I've seen that on your computer. It's your screen-saver."

"Right. Handy when I go into tech hell."

We talked about things that had gone wrong with our computers for a while, then he said, "Oh, I know another Atisha slogan that might help with your mother."

"Oh? What?"

"'Don't expect applause.'"

EIGHT

They Used to Call Me God, but They'll Never Call Me Buddha

THIS MORNING, I got a postcard from my friend Sally in the English department, a picture of a palm-lined stretch of white beach. "Really envy you all that quiet and peace, but aren't you ever coming home? We miss you."

The fall quarter at the university had come and gone without me. There was too much to do at Dorje Ling to even think about leaving. A few phone calls was all it took to burn my bridges. Now my family and friends seemed to think that I occupied a blissful cocoon, lapped round with serenity and love.

What did they know? How could I explain that these past six months at Dorje Ling had been the most challenging of my whole life, that moments of quiet and peace were few and as rare as daytime stars. Furthermore, hard as I worked physically, it seemed a vacation compared to my hard-hat level of mental activity. Everything I had ever thought, every hang-up and habit, turned this way and that until underlying assumptions yielded up their patterns and distortions, their hooked claws of attachment.

In my childhood, my grandfather once gave me a microscope and let me make slides out of anything I wanted: a flower, a fly's wing, a bit of bread dough, a piece of yarn. Understanding that there were levels and levels of vision affected me profoundly, leading me to daydream that by twisting my ear, I could turn my eyes into microscopes, enabling me to see through whatever baffled me. I felt that at Dorje Ling, I'd turned such a microscope back on myself but had been unprepared for its disclosures.

I think a lot about anger these days. How the commercial kitchen used to run on rage. How appropriate it felt to indulge in tirades about what should or shouldn't be done. I'd seen anger as a divine dance, something I'd earned a right to express. Besides, hadn't I worked my way up from kitchen help by being unrelentingly precise and demanding in every detail? Hadn't I made a point of never faltering in my zealous control of both the process and the product? Anger released adrenaline, energy, force. It kept the kitchen going. But at Dorje Ling I discovered that it has a big price tag hanging from its toe. People dislike you afterward, so you have to keep feeling angry, keep feeding it, keep pushing that energy outward in order not to wind up with the letdown, not to take in the effects of your anger on other people.

Lama Tashi once said that when someone gets angry at you, it's as if they were shooting arrows. If you respond with more anger, it is as if you picked up the arrows that fell at your feet and proceeded to stab yourself over and over.

A cook isn't necessarily angry, but a chef is almost always furious on some level. Why? Will. Control and perfection. Professional entitlement. And what happens to all of this anger in the kitchen at a Buddhist center? To begin with, it starts to feel like damage rather than privilege. I would track the impact of anger, follow its effects on myself and others. I noted my racing heart, narrowed eyes, intense concentration outward onto something that others, *they,* were doing wrong. An inner dialogue raged over flaws, the rightness of my position, my method, my perfect food, my idea of how a dish should look, should taste. In short, I concentrated on myself, my own assumptions. I would take what was inside my head, project it outward—reify it—think it was real in itself. I'm right, *they* are wrong. Puff, puff. But the center of energy still raged on inside my own being.

That in itself, I came to realize, isn't the whole problem. When I engage with anger, nothing else can happen. Nothing. No love. No joy. Only rage. And it feeds itself. It comes in waves, say the psychologists. The first wave of anger tends to be fairly mild, but then, after we've pumped it up a bit, after we've fanned the flames with words and memories of earlier outrages, it becomes stronger, deeper, meaner.

I soon found that getting in touch with rage as a source of power, as the self-help books advise, doesn't work except in the very short term. When I really began to watch the effects of my words, I saw that anger couldn't do me or anyone else a bit of good. But how to control it?

I ask Lama P. when he comes into the kitchen to melt coconut oil for butter lamps. Dorje Ling buys the oil in five-gallon tins from somewhere in Thailand. When visitors melt the oil, they tend to mess up the stove, slopping it over the burners, creating a real fire hazard. This particular lama never spills a drop.

"So, what do you do with anger? Stuff it?"

"Watch it. Feel it without acting on it. Don't identify with it. See it as a poison. Different from stuffing it. Watch it. Oil's melted, got to go."

Lama P. picks up the huge pot of hot oil and heads toward the porch where he's already set out the butter lamps, each with a wick in the gobletlike brass holders.

One thing about this center, the one with lamas rather than horses, they don't spoon-feed you, they throw you into the deep end. Sink or swim. Whatever personal assistance I get, I usually receive on the fly, while working by the stove. I sometimes watch the lamas with the newbies, answering questions, being patient, kind, loving. I remember those days, but I'm not a newbie anymore. I'm supposed to know what's what.

My eyes narrow and my heart begins to race as I think about how much better the newbies are treated than I am. Even though I work long hours in the kitchen while some of them just sit around soaking up the sun, chatting up the lamas. Pretty useless in the kitchen, too, most of these new people.

Oh, grow up, a voice in my head interrupts my looming rant about what is wrong with others. Blaming *them*—the administration, the center, the lamas—for not giftwrapping the answers and presenting them tied with a bow to precious little me. But, in fact, I *have* been given all of the teachings on the emotional poisons—ignorance, anger, attachment, pride, and jealousy—over and over again. Even with Lama P.'s most recent concise instruction, I'd listened at first, but then a deeply entrenched habit began to color my response, leading me to seek out and dwell on the faults of others. By concentrating on the newbies, I'd distanced myself from taking in, from applying the teachings where they were most needed—in my own mind.

Oh, I sighed deeply, growing up is hard. And endless.

After the first month, I'd gone to Lama Tashi in tears, saying that I was hopeless, that my mind seethed and wriggled with poisons, that I had the attention of a flea, the motivation of a cat. Hopeless, just hopeless.

He'd smiled very kindly, nodded cheerfully. Oh, yes, he agreed, my mind had always been hopelessly out of control, but I just hadn't noticed. Now I was beginning to pay attention. This was a good sign. "Progress having" was the way he put it.

Dealing with food management in a retreat center was in some ways no different from working in any kitchen. I looked around the kitchen at Dorje Ling. There's heat, mess, perishable materials, deadlines, difficult or un-trained people, et cetera. What's different? The need to watch your mind. Me, I corrected myself. For *me* to watch *my* mind, not yours. Your mind is none of my business. What is of concern is to stop creating harm, learn to be helpful. And not just when it's convenient, but all the time. I was finding that this journey from anger to com-passion is one I took baby-step by baby-step.

Untying the knots of anger is just like making a com-plicated meal. Even when one understands all of the techniques, has assembled all of the recipes and ingredients in a working kitchen, a person still has to work through the entire cooking process in correct order, being careful not to miss a step. You can't just think the meal onto the table, can't talk it into existence.

And even when you've created a complex, perfect meal—or worked through to the roots of anger—you still have to go through all of the steps again the next time. And the next. And the next.

I'm only five minutes late for the teaching, although I could well have stayed in bed longer since no one is there when I arrive. A Tibetan teacher might turn up five minutes early or an hour late. Then he might keep talking for three hours longer than scheduled. Or stay up with you half the night drinking beer and telling stories. The Tibetans I'd met all had a sort of wild, unpredictable energy that pulled you right into the present moment with them.

This Tibetan is a young *khenpo,* or scholar. Raised and educated at Rumtek Monastery in Sikkim, he hasn't been inside Tibet itself since he was six years old. The translator, a bespectacled English monk in a red robe who travels with the *khenpo,* is fussy about all of the details surrounding the talk. It takes quite a while for him to get the cushions right, the tea thermos situated, the stage set.

When the *khenpo* starts talking, I can't understand a word he says. I can't even understand the translation. The *khenpo's* voice is soothing, like a river, going on and on. By the time the Englishman interprets, so much teaching has passed that I can't remember what has gone before. He's talking about emptiness and I try hard to listen, but the words keep jumbling themselves up. Something about the four extremes, emptiness is beyond either/or and neither/nor, beyond neither either/or and neither/nor, and beyond . . .

Sitting propped up against the back wall, I'm struggling to stay awake, fighting the cold medicine only part of the problem. I take back everything I said about the wild, unpredictable energy of the Tibetans.

"So the self," I hear someone asking the question when I jerk awake, "is like a weather system?" How long had I slept? How did they get from neither/nor to this weather system thing?

"A weather system that changes minute by minute so that you can't really pinpoint it as something real and solid? Yet it's there, it's happening. Constantly in flux, unstable. A sort of ongoing, impermanent event. Is that right?"

The Englishman translated the question, the *khenpo* talked on and on, and by the time his answer came into English, I had drifted off again. I wasn't sure, but I thought the *khenpo* said yes, it was. It was like a weather system.

NINE

Soup

AS I STIR the soup it occurs to me how much more co-operative vegetables are than people, especially when it comes to blending together and creating a whole. Vegetables cooperate into soup; people together is another story entirely, although here in Buddha's kitchen we all at least try to get along, to work together, to cooperate like vegetables in the soup. Carrots don't swim to the surface saying, "Look, look. I'm a carrot, I'm the most important thing in the soup." They just add flavor and nourishment to the stock. Nor does mushroom-barley soup strut around saying that it tastes better than yesterday's *yaki-soba*. People could learn a lot from vegetables, from being part of the soup.

The most intensely involved I've ever been with soup was when I wrote a play called *Dragon Soup & Other Intense Sensations*. It was produced in a local restaurant that served the same menu to the audience as was being prepared in the play itself. Staged all over the restaurant, the action sometimes could be seen only through the large wall mirrors. For the kitchen scenes, we pulled a prep table onto the postage-stamp clearing we used for a stage.

The waiters' station doubled as the actors' green room for the six weeks that the play ran. We found that to put the production's mess of lights and props on top of a restaurant's normal mess was too much for everyone, but we learned to cope. After casting, the director decided to write cabaret music for the production, then went around giving singing lessons. I played a character named Blanche, a plant at one of the front tables, who cooed rather than talked when the waiter presented the menu to her. By the end, few of the staff members of the restaurant were speaking to the cast of the play except for those who were sleeping together. Nonetheless, the play ran for weeks and had over a hundred people on the waiting list when it closed.

The play was based on the restaurant where I'd started as kitchen help and ended up as dinner chef. (It wasn't that hard; battles are often pitched in restaurant kitchens, then whoever is left standing gets promoted.)

In writing the play, I was surprised at how much the character of Chef was a purified form of the real-life luncheon chef at Lafayette's, a woman I'll call Rocky. But just as the five poisons become the five wisdoms when perfected, so Chef is a sort of perfected Rocky.

Here's how the soup in *Dragon Soup* comes about:

ACT 1, SCENE 2

[Lunch is over. Lighting is very dim. Kitchen has the air of an animal's den, yellow and dark like an underground cavern where perhaps primitive rituals are enacted. A few candles burn here and there.

CHEF, very dark, perhaps brown or black, is a huge woman, more of a force of nature than a human being. Odd things hang from her here and there, perhaps a string of sausages or a rope of garlic. One wouldn't be surprised to see a live snake. She alone can see DRAGON.]

CHEF: Better get to work on the soup. [*passing by spices, she points finger accusingly*] Don't you talk back to me. Had enough of you I have ... You juniper berries. Perk up there, got things for you to do tonight. Big things.

Now you, you pretty mushrooms. What you in the mood for today? Marjoram? Oregano? Little beauties, you are. So white and round. [*she turns on a cassette recorder (African drums or perhaps Ravel's Bolero), she hits pot with a wooden spoon, breaks into a dance, bouncing heavily*]

CHEF: Dum de de dum de de. [*dances*] Dum de de dum de de.

Soup, soup, gonna make some soup. [*calls*] Dragon. Hey Dragon. Dragooooooonnnnnn. [*crosses to broom closet, throws open door. DRAGON, sitting on stool writing, pays no attention to her*] Dragon. [*waits respectfully*] HEY, DRAGON.

DRAGON: [*still writing*] Um?

CHEF: Dragon. Needs your help. You busy?

DRAGON: [*coming out of closet*] Just working on a poem. What's up?

CHEF: Needs to get the Chef's Special.

DRAGON: Ah, the Chef's Special. [*sniffing; CHEF too begins to sniff*] What sort of day is it?

CHEF: [*sniffing*] Well, [*sniffs*] sort of . . . [*sniff, sniff*] kinda . . . [*sniffs*] Know what I mean?

DRAGON: [*sniffs*] A spicy sort of day.

CHEF: Yeah, ginger spicy.

DRAGON: Many surprises.

CHEF: Oh, boy. Loves surprises.

DRAGON: [*as if he's looking into the day*] Hmmmmm-mmm.

CHEF: What's you mean "Hmmmmmmmm?"

DRAGON: Just Hmm. Great spectrum of surprises.

CHEF: [*to herself*] Spec Trum.

DRAGON: Reminds me a little of the day I came through. [*sniffs deeply*] Yes, indeed. [*beat*] The day I came through and couldn't get back.

CHEF: [*who loves to hear DRAGON talk*] That the day of the big earthquake?

DRAGON: The very same. I'd only come in for dinner that night.

CHEF: How's the food?

DRAGON: Oh! Even then it was worth traveling for.

CHEF: [*very childlike; she's heard this story many times*] Yeah? What'd you have?

DRAGON: We started with Winter Melon Soup.

CHEF: We? [*her favorite part is about the other dragon, the one who got lost*]

DRAGON: [*sadly*] My dragon and I.

CHEF: Yeah?

DRAGON: Yeah. [*turns stoical*] Then BANG. Everything changed.

CHEF: BANG! Loves to happen.

DRAGON: Winter Melon Soup all over everywhere, plaster falling, then the fire . . . smoke and confusion.

CHEF: Yeah? And?

DRAGON: When it was all over, I was alone and the co-ordinate point sealed off—no more traveling between dimensions. Can't get back at all. [*shakes head*] Now there's a broom closet where the entry point used to be. Don't know if she made it or not.

CHEF: Your dragon?

DRAGON: For years I thought maybe she just went into shock, forgot who she was. Dragons do that. They enter the dream . . . [*lost in reverie*]

CHEF: Now, 'bout that soup.

DRAGON: Ah, yes, the soup. [*begins to intone*] Eeeeeeee eessssscccccooooffffffiiiiiaaayyy. Eeeeeessssccccooooffffiiiiaaayyy. Escoffier. Escoffier.

CHEF: That's today's soup?

DRAGON: Wait. [*intones again*] O Great Chefs of France, speak through me. [*bangs pots and pans*] O mighty caul-drons, bubble for me. [*makes stylized gestures*] Deep pleasures, dark pleasures . . . Ah. Take fruits, heavy on the vine, swollen by the sun into ruby globes.

CHEF: [*writing down recipe on card*] Them's ripe toma-toes. Calls 'em fruits. Don't never 'frigerate.

DRAGON: Minced root of the golden flower, plucked young from Dragon's garden. To clear the mind, to shock the senses beyond the limits of the body, into the clarity of the void.

CHEF: Guess that's ginger root.

DRAGON: That amber liquid, that transformed aura of the plump fowl, prepared by the light of the East.

CHEF: [*flips through file box, takes out card, and reads aloud*] Chinese chicken stock. Okay. Got that.

DRAGON: The spring offering of green, grown long and thin, reaching out of the soil, gently biting to the tongue as a lover with tiny pointy teeth . . .

CHEF: Scallions!

DRAGON: [*who had not quite finished; coughs politely*] Hem.

CHEF: Sorry.

DRAGON: As a lover with tiny, pointy teeth might naughtily bite. Brought to their fullest potential in the high, hot world to the south, amid explosive darkness.

CHEF: [*impressed*] Done up with salsa.

[*Enter WAITER, brushing DRAGON aside*]

WAITER: Chef. Chef.

DRAGON: Oh, bother. Humans! And I was just getting started. Hmph. [*DRAGON goes back into closet*]

WAITER: Got to get the Chef's Special for the menu. What's all this?

CHEF: That's gonna be soup.

WAITER: [*pencil poised*] Name?

CHEF: Name?

WAITER: Name of the soup.

CHEF: Name of the soup. Uh. Didn't give me no name.

WAITER: What?

CHEF: Um, nothing. The name . . . uh . . . it's . . . uh.

WAITER: Jeez. Not again. [*sigh*] Maybe I can help. Salsa? Ginger root? Chinese chicken stock? How about UNESCO Surprise?

[*CHEF nods enthusiastically until she realizes that WAITER, a French snob at heart, is being sarcastic. DRAGON appears briefly from closet*]

DRAGON: Crab meat might be even better.

CHEF: [*calling*] Dragon . . . [*sees look on WAITER's face and finishes*] Soup.

WAITER: What?

CHEF: Dragon Soup. That's the name of the soup. The Chef's Special for tonight.

WAITER: Is that so?

CHEF: Yes, write it down just like that: Dragon Soup.

WAITER: Tell me, Cheffie, is it made from dragon meat? The customers will ask, you know.

CHEF: No, course it ain't. Dragon give me the recipe.

WAITER: Of course he did, darling. Of course he did.

At the end of the play, it turns out that the chef is the dragon's lost mate. Once he recognizes her own true nature as well as his own, they are able to return to their original dimension.

TEN

Kitchen Talk

ONE OF THE THINGS I like about working in a kitchen, any kitchen, is the talk. It seems to have a quality all its own. When I was growing up, my sense of community came from a kitchen full of busy women working together. During holidays, in my great-aunt's huge old house in South Carolina, the older along with the duller members of the family would gather in the formal living room. There, self-conscious and overly polite, I had to sit stiff and straight. As soon as possible I'd escape to the large kitchen, with its brick floor and fireplace, once a separate building but by then attached to the house through a screened passageway. A domain apart, the kitchen off Aunt Hattie's porch held rich, wet smells, action, warmth. And connection. Cousins, aunts, and grandmothers surrounded me with a large, warm tide of female flesh and noise: talking, gossiping, giving advice, counsel, with voices that seemed to take up half an acre each.

My mother always stayed in the living room with the thin women who offered dry kisses to the air near a cheek. But the females in the kitchen planted juicy smacks, swooped me up in enormous hugs, bestowed spontaneous squeezes, pats, playful pinches. In the midst of this great seething mass of extended family, my aunts and women cousins were always telling me what to think, what to wear, how to behave. Advice, hints, and life plans were slipped into platters of benne seed wafers and angel biscuits, tucked into chicken casseroles, lemon pies, raspberry jelly.

I loved the secrets that were revealed in that steamy holiday kitchen, the truth behind the family's polite shadow play—Aunt Margaret's cancer, Henry's drinking, Felicia's too-quick wedding—whatever went unmentioned, unmentionable in the dining room, would be displayed, analyzed, clucked over, even with me standing right below them, my nose barely to the tabletop. At last my mother's coded language made sense and I would be able to stitch together the person and the event that Mother had been describing in the secret language of Victorian-raised women. But here in the kitchen, women, packed into girdles, aprons over their silk print dresses, would let me decorate a salad plate, arrange lemon cookies and butterscotch brownies on a crystal tray, fill nut cups even as they provided the best gossip in town. Their darting hands opened this lid, then that, cracking the oven door to check on the browning sweet potato casserole and the yeast rolls, retying a passing child's hair bow or sash. Yet none would miss a single detail of the several involved stories mulled over at once across the stove and around the table.

The women of the family pretended to defer to their men, but in fact they never did. In reality, the men were simply pushed to the periphery, sitting patiently together like survivors of a hurricane. When my aunts and cousins finally heard about women's liberation, they'd asked, "What for? I just don't see the point."

Very few conversations are ever finished in a restaurant, at least not among the staff. At Lafayette's, I learned to put conversations on hold and to finish a sentence or answer a question after one to two hours. There is something about a restaurant kitchen, or maybe it was just Lafayette's kitchen, that made people come in and spill their guts to perfect strangers about their daughter's abortion, their husband's impotence. I saw it happen over and over: "Here, lady, here's the tomatoes you ordered. On a date last night, this woman, Bunny's her name, well, Bunny and I . . ."

This at ten in the morning.

In the afternoons, the chef, Jules, and I would talk endlessly about food as we got dinner ready. In one session, standing across from each other at the prep table, we might prepare onion soup, basil dressing, chicken Dijon, pilaf, coquilles St. Jacques, artichoke hearts and béarnaise sauce for the tournedos, marinated Italian vegetables, carrots Vichy, a Sacher torte, Bavarian cream, and French chocolate cake.

That night, all would be portioned out, served up, garnished, sent out, devoured.

The next day, on the same prep we would cut up mushrooms for one soup, dice ginger and scallions for another. We'd mix up a stuffing for trout, pound veal pieces until they were thin, glaze a roast pork, season the pepper beef, make a chocolate mousse, roll out tart shells, and zest the lemons to go in the filling.

The menu changed every day and was completely

subject to Jules's whim. Unlike Rocky's messing, everything Jules cooked tasted good. And he liked to experiment.

My most unrelenting pleasure at Lafayette's was the necessity to taste everything being prepared, many times. All day long I'd get to dip my finger in the hollandaise, to lick the spoon I'd used to mix the Grand Marnier sauce, to scrape out the whipped cream bowl, to break off the edge of a quiche as I dished it up—in short, to nibble and graze throughout the day.

Jules and I talked mostly about food. "Did you hear," he'd say as he put an aspic glaze on a chicken, building up the layers so that he could embed flowers cut out of carrots with stems and leaves of chives, "about the man who won that big food presentation contest in France last year? Well, I'm not sure he won, but nobody talked about anything else. He did a shark, a whole seven-foot-long shark. He built a pit to cook it in, had to cook it for like four days, then he put little pilot fish and bits of seaweed all over it. Everybody else was livid. There they were with their little jellied eels and decorated chickens and he had this mammoth shark!"

Or we would argue various merits of this or that technique or ingredient. Did the hollandaise taste better if we whipped the butter in with a whisk rather than using the blender? Could people *really* tell the difference if we started with canned chicken stock rather than cooking down a broth ourselves? (The answer to this was no.) Could we tell the difference? Usually not, especially in cream soups where so much was added to the stock. Was the slight difference in taste worth all the extra trouble and expense? Where did gourmet stop and idiocy begin?

The sauces were a revelation to me. As a southerner, I'd been raised on white sauce or gravy and didn't think much of either. Later, as I cooked my way up the university ladder, I'd learned about hollandaise and béarnaise, but the whole family of sauces built on a demi-glace base—from bordelaise to diable to Robert—opened up an unsuspected range of subtleties. Sauces were Jules's specialty, and I loved to watch him with his beautiful face serious, almost reverent, as he intently connected with the progress of his sauce. Even on bad days (and there were plenty), he'd get back to normal if he had a complicated sauce to create.

We would often read recipes from cookbooks from the restaurant's wide selection. At times we read to get ideas for dinner, at other times just for the pleasure. "Listen to this," I'd say. "Potage Pierre-le-Grand, or Peter the Great Soup: 'This soup can be made by mixing mushroom and hazel-grouse purees.' Hazel-grouse puree? We haven't used up the rest of the hazel-grouse puree, have we? Oh, here's a good one: Partridge in Tangerine Cups. Do you think the lunch crowd would give up their ham sandwiches for that?" And so on.

Sometimes Jules and I would talk about Virginia Woolf, for we were both avid fans. We copied out a passage from *A Room of One's Own* to hang over the sink: "The human frame being what it is, heart, body and brain all mixed together, and not contained in separate compartments as they will be no doubt in another million years, a good dinner is of great importance to good talk. One cannot think well, love well, sleep well, if one has not dined well."

As time went on, I began to stay later and later each afternoon. After a few months, I began to work three or four nights a week as Jules's sous-chef. Dinner had a much more stately progression than lunch. Food was more carefully presented, the service was better, and the menu had a balance and harmony lacking at the midday meal. Lafayette's offered soup, salad, entrée, and dessert for one price. Each night—and they served dinner every night except Sunday and Monday—they would have two soups, three salads, three or four entrées, and three desserts. If the customers wanted, they could order à la carte, but most chose to take the entire meal. Since we started serving around six and usually wouldn't take any orders past nine-thirty, we fed fewer people than at lunch, although each person ate more. At night, Lafayette's patrons didn't simply eat, they dined.

And dined lavishly. In the kitchen, we were able to pour all of our attention, will, and expertise into each dish, each presentation. We'd sometimes watch people eat, wait for that moment when their eyes went wide after trying something, when they'd sit up a little straighter, bend toward the food, and nibble again. My God, their bodies would say, I didn't know food could taste like that!

Then Jules and I would open a bottle of Fleurie and propose a toast.

"To good food," we'd say, knowing that all of the very hard work of the afternoon had paid off. "To dining well."

ELEVEN

Jizo Ceremony

WE SAT in a circle making small red bibs.

"Jizo Ceremony for Aborted and Miscarried Children," read the large hand-lettered sign behind the registration desk of the Buddhist Women's Conference in San Francisco.

"I'm not going," a woman beside me at the registration desk had said aloud earlier, though no one had asked. Now I sat across from her, her head bent over scraps of red cloth.

The ceremony was led by a Zen teacher from Florida. She seemed stern, businesslike, almost severe. She'd begun the session by telling us that we'd make bibs for an aborted or miscarried child (or children), then, in a group ceremony at the end, offer the bibs to Jizo, the *bodhisattva* who guides unborn children through the underworld. A *bodhisattva,* she explained, is dedicated to helping others and has vowed not to pass into nirvana until everyone is enlightened.

Red cloth, scissors, thread, needles were laid out on work tables. Once we assembled the materials, we were supposed to sit in a circle and talk as we made the bibs. The activity of cutting out the cloth, finding who had the spool of thread, an extra needle, helped to channel the nervous and sometimes fearful energy that kept building in the room. Sitting in a circle, sewing, this grounded us, sank us into a tradition we felt in our bodies even if we'd never experienced it directly in our busy modern lives before.

In Japan, the teacher said, where abortion is very widespread, statues of Jizo are common. At many shrines, children's clothing—little coats, bibs, dresses—and toys are heaped high. Through the open door out on the grass, we could see a two-foot statue of this *bodhisattva* made of stone.

The teacher, who didn't seem severe once she began talking, spoke for a while about abortion, then grew quiet. We sewed in silence. Then a woman near me began, in a flat voice.

"I've had three abortions."

"Two," another woman added.

"I'm still pro-choice," a woman said a little defensively. Several women—including me—nodded.

An academic woman who'd seemed stiff and guarded at a workshop earlier in the day began to speak. "I'm pro-choice, too." Her voice wavered and cracked. "I'll always be pro-choice. My abortion was the result of a rape."

Pain—shared, visceral pain—swept the room.

"I had two abortions in my early twenties." A slim, gray-haired woman spoke. "I didn't know that those would be the only times I'd ever be pregnant."

After a short silence an older woman named Joan spoke, "My oldest daughter had two abortions in her early twenties. I found out about them afterward, and not from her." She had cut out three bibs: two tiny ones to tuck inside a larger one. "I was forty-seven—my three girls finally raised and out of the house—I couldn't go through all that again. Didn't want to. I was just thankful abortions are legal now. They hadn't been when I'd gotten pregnant at nineteen. I'd had to marry—so it seemed at the time. Not that the marriage lasted."

A writer whose work had influenced and helped many of the women there started to speak, stopped, then started again. "We were in Iran when I miscarried. Twin girls. If I'd come back to the States they might have had a chance. But I didn't. They would have been thirty years old last week."

Again a wave of pain. I felt my heart squeeze, my throat tighten, eyes blur. Such ancient pain carried by the mother line.

The older woman, Joan, began speaking again. "I'd never thought of my daughter's abortions as missing grandchildren before. Grandchildren I'll never hold. She'd been married—but angry at her husband—for the second one. She didn't tell him about it till after the divorce. Heartless.

"My own abortion brought my partner and me closer together. We were in danger of splitting apart at the time. Separation seemed certain, but we found each other again through the experience of the abortion. We've been together now for over fifteen years, stable, happy.

"He would have been a little boy," Joan told us. "He would have loved me in a simple, direct way that my oldest daughter never had, never could. She was always tormenting me, herself. What is this karma between mothers and daughters? Why so much rage? Where does this fury come from?"

A younger woman in a blue vest spoke up. "I didn't want a baby; I didn't want to be like my mother," she said as if following Joan's train of thought. Other women spoke up, saying more or less the same thing. There was a confused sense of women trying to abort their mothers, not their children.

"I am ashamed," a beautiful Asian woman in the circle said, "that I didn't ask permission from the fetus. Afterward I went to a healer and he said to do that. If you're thinking of having an abortion, talk to the fetus, explain your situation. Ask the baby to come at another time. Now I counsel my patients to do this. Very often they report a spontaneous abortion."

Again a palpable wave of pain rose in the room. We were united in something timeless. I had never felt such a sense of shared anguish, of a common physical experience that went too deep for words. Personal distress transmuted into group suffering. I no longer knew whose pain I was feeling.

"We wanted the baby so much." A woman with very short hair spoke. The woman beside her, her partner, placed a hand over the speaker's womb. "We'd planned it for years. We had to wait until we'd saved enough money, then we had to find a suitable donor. It took several tries for me to finally get pregnant. Then we were so happy." She started crying. Her partner, also crying, began to speak.

"It seemed a miracle that we'd be able to have a child at last, be parents. Only . . ." She couldn't talk any more.

"The miscarriage hurt so much. It still hurts. Physically, I mean, as well as every other way. The pain never stops."

Name the fetus, the workshop leader said. Name the fetus and talk to it before you say goodbye. The room went silent except for the sounds of sobbing.

Late in the afternoon, the teacher rose, led us outside to stand in a circle around the statue of Jizo. One by one we went up to the statue, bowed, placed a bib around his neck, and bowed again. The last time, the whole group bowed.

"Thank you, Jizo," I said silently when it was my turn. "Thank you for taking care of the little ones that we didn't want, the ones we lost or threw away."

Some of us cried as we put bibs around the statue's neck, others looked clear, cleansed. As we bowed in unison, we acknowledged each woman's act, each woman's loss, guilt, pain. Each child seemed to be our own as we said goodbye and gave it over to the care of the *bodhisattva*.

TWELVE

Impermanence

A WOMAN from New York arrived at Dorje Ling early in the week, her red Blazer packed with stacks of notebooks, leather bags stuffed with papers, cameras, and tripods. A tiny dog named Lhasa-la sat curled on the front seat. She had come to interview the Tibetans for a book she was writing on the loss of their country.

I had no idea that Lama Nyingpo, the little monk who smiled at me so sweetly when I brought him a lunch tray, had spent ten years in a prison camp, that he was repeatedly tortured and almost starved to death. When I brought his food, he always beamed at me, thanked me profusely, went out of his way to smile and nod. Yet this same man lost his monastery in Tibet, watched it being blown up by the Chinese, saw hundreds of his fellow monks die, his family wiped out.

"I complain when anyone comes in and tries to talk to me while I'm cooking," I said to Lama P., "but what if someone came into the kitchen and started shooting the way the Chinese did in the Tibetan monasteries? What if the kitchen itself were gone, blown up? I can't imagine what it's like for a Tibetan to watch us in the States."

"Especially here in California," Lama P. said. "Lama Tashi once told us that we might rate our suffering on the scale of 1 to 10, but the real scale goes from 1 to 100 and we just don't know it."

Lama Nyingpo had given the group a teaching once on impermanence, on how you can't count on anything being around for very long, on how we should be happy with each other just because we're here together in this beautiful place. Life is uncertain. You never know if you're going to have another day. But he never mentioned Tibet, prison, his blown-up monastery, the torture, his dead family. When something bad happens to me, I realized, I tell everyone, usually several times. But Lama Nyingpo never mentioned himself or his own losses, just that we should be more careful with each other, that we should appreciate what we have in the moment. That the moment is all we have.

People, I thought as I watched the hot bubbles come to the surface and break as I stirred the stew, are as impermanent as these bubbles, rising and popping, rising and popping. Yet I feel—not just think, but actually feel deep in my body—that I *am* permanent, real and solid. Despite all the evidence to the contrary. Other people die, but I'm going to keep on forever and ever.

Only recently had I perceived tiny fissures in my own sense of ongoing solidity. Glimpses into something Out There that didn't exclude me, but just wasn't based on me. Unlike in the stories of the great yogis, this hadn't occurred on my cushion during formal meditation sessions—few things happened there except misery—but as I'd been walking across the broad grassy field in front of the main building at Dorje Ling. Just a sudden glimpse into . . . what? I had no name for it. Just this inner coming together that allowed something to open, creating a clear channel for some sort of expanded perception.

I gave up trying to analyze what I'd seen or how it had come into being. I just tried to remember the sudden shift in the universe when everything was just startlingly *there*.

I felt a pressure against my leg. Julie, Lynn's little girl, pressed up against me, rubbing her forehead back and forth against the side of my apron.

"You're part cat, you know that, Julie?"

"Ummhummm." Rub. Rub.

My hand rested lightly on the little blonde head, stroking her tangled hair. Julie grabbed my hand, turned it over and kissed it, then skipped off.

"Nothing like a little visit from an angel." Diane and I watched Julie go to the door, hop over the sill, jump back again, then out the door. She did this funny double-hop whenever she left the kitchen by that particular door. In fact, the child was full of small rituals, tiny repeated movements and gestures. She rarely talked, and if anyone asked her why she'd done something, she'd throw her jacket over her head and rush away, blushing furiously.

Fey was the word that always came to my mind in connection with Julie. It was also almost the last word that I'd connect with another child at Dorje Ling, the young Tulku Purba. I had never heard of a *tulku* until I'd moved there. It was one of those Tibetan things I could never quite either accept or reject. The basic idea was that a lama—almost always a male—would decide to reincarnate again as a teacher, then be recognized as a reincarnation—a *tulku*—when a child and raised accordingly.

Certainly the *tulkus* who came to Dorje Ling had a special air, a particular kind of energy that was unique. If you went along with reincarnation, that much was okay. But then my feminism would kick in and not fail to notice that it functioned as a way for childless monks to control and perpetuate their own lineage without including wives or women. Once I started thinking about this, my mind would boil and bubble with poison, remembering all the bad things I'd heard about lamaism and its abuses in Tibet.

But only that morning, Lama Tashi had told us about his first encounter with a watch in Tibet. He'd never seen one before when a friend came by with a wristwatch he'd just bought from a trader. "It's wonderful," the friend said. "You wind it up and it will tell you exactly when you are going to die. So you can prepare."

Maybe good reminder, he said he'd thought at the time, to keep death strapped to your wrist. Later, when the same friend told him of a small box that let you hear the voices of people two valleys away, he didn't believe him. When someone else added that you could get a box like that, but bigger, that had pictures as well, Lama Tashi felt sorry that anyone would tell that sort of lie to a lama. You find the same sort of outraged disbelief—well founded in cultural ignorance—when Westerners hear about reincarnation for the first time.

Recently, I had learned to let a number of things just

sort of lie there in my mind without either accepting or rejecting them. Lama S. told me that this was an improvement, this new ability not to rush to judgment and quick rejection of things I really didn't know anything about.

At any rate, the *tulku* thing was large at Dorje Ling and nowhere larger than with Tulku Purba, a little boy once named Joey. His mother, who worked in the office, still called him this when she got mad. Once trying to get something done, one of the carpenters had tied Tulku Purba to the steering wheel of his truck until he could finish what should have taken five minutes but what, with the boy's "help," had stretched on for hours. "Great idea," his mother said later. "Save me the rope."

In the kitchen, we had to follow certain rules with Tulku Purba. Never touch him on the top of his head. Always feed him on the special dishes set aside for the lamas. Treat him with respect.

"Little shit," Lynn sometimes said to his back when he'd pull her daughter Julie's hair, then run off laughing. "Tulku Turd."

"There is something wrong with Julie." Tulku Purba stood at the kitchen door looking unusually doubtful. Normally, everything he said or did overflowed with confidence if not arrogance.

Lynn was already out the door.

Drubchen—ten days of intense practice—was coming up. Almost a hundred visitors were expected, so everyone in the kitchen had been working double and triple time trying to get ready. Lynn, the gofer this time around, had been in Redding most of the week, her blue truck tearing around the mountain curves as she tried to beat her own best time of forty-two minutes.

Lonny, who had gone to the hospital with Lynn and Julie, called later from the emergency room. "They don't know what's wrong. Julie's having seizures of some sort."

"Seizures?"

"They've got to run some tests. Maybe take her down to San Francisco. It's horrible. Put her on the prayer list."

Everybody came together in the middle of the kitchen, scared, confused. Bad things weren't supposed to happen. Suddenly everyone wanted to touch, to hug, to feel the comfort of another person's body. Over Diane's shoulder, I saw Tulku Purba standing near the door, eyes round, mouth open.

"Tulku-la is so worried about Julie," his mother said the next day. Julie was still in the local hospital under observation. "He keeps asking how she is."

"Compassion showing," Lama Tashi beamed. "Good sign."

I wasn't so sure, but didn't say anything.

"Come here a minute," I called to the little boy when I saw him hanging around the kitchen later that afternoon. Growing up, I'd played with my boy cousins enough to know when something was up.

"I have to go finish my practice." He tried to slink away, a sure sign.

"In a minute." I held on to him. "Tell me what happened with Julie."

"She was just lying there on the ground and couldn't

get up. Her eyes just sort of rolled around in her head."
He demonstrated.

"Yes, I know that. But what happened last week." Stab
in the dark.

"Nothing." All innocence.

"I mean when Lynn was in Redding the other day."

I could feel him struggle. I'd asked the right question.
"It may be important."

"You mean when she got hit in the head with the
baseball?"

It turned out that Julie had been running past the baseball
field when a fly ball had bopped her. A visitor named Ben
had hit the ball. The whole thing was an accident. She'd
fallen down, cried, then gotten up and run away. Evidently
she hadn't told Lynn. Since Ben wasn't supposed to be
there—his father objected to him being on Buddhist
land—Tulku Purba had kept quiet about it as well, then
forgotten it had happened until Julie went to the hospital.

"She's going to be okay, isn't she?" He had tears in his
eyes. "Isn't she?"

"I hope so," I told him, reaching for the phone, obscurely
grateful that he hadn't been the one to hit that fly ball.

"The doctor said to watch her. It is probably the result of
being hit," Lynn reported to the kitchen after dinner.
"Julie's back at home. She seems okay."

The kitchen gave a collective sigh of relief. "Thank
goodness it isn't anything really serious."

But we were dead wrong about that.

"Epilepsy?"

"That's what the doctor said." Lonny was calling from San Francisco.

"What about the hit with the baseball?"

"He thinks maybe that set it off."

"Is Julie going to be all right?"

"The doctor didn't have much time to talk to us, but they've given her this medication. She hasn't had a seizure since then."

"What about Lynn?"

"She's okay, I guess. But you know Lynn, she's so macho sometimes."

In the months to come, Lynn's macho control slipped, fell, shattered. A new drug would work for a while, then suddenly stop doing any good. Julie would get sick after each seizure. She couldn't eat, began to lose weight.

Julie didn't start school that fall. She was to have been in the second grade. The staff at Dorje Ling took turns sitting with her in the afternoons so Lynn could do errands. One afternoon, when I hadn't seen her in a week or more, I was shocked at how thin the child had become.

"You're all eyes, Sweet Pea," I told Julie.

"You're all curly hair," she answered, giggling. Then burrowed her blushing face into my shoulder.

"It's just not fair," Diane cried in despair. "Not fair at all. Julie's getting worse. I don't know if I can stand it."

Lama S. happened to be walking through the kitchen at the time, but came to a dead halt when Diane said that. I had heard of Lama S. being wrathful but never witnessed it. I instinctively stepped back as she whipped around toward the prep table.

"Diane, what is the first noble truth?"

"Life is suffering, but . . ."

"But nothing. Look at me. Do you think because we're living in a Buddhist center we have some sort of special deal with the universe that bad things won't happen to us?"

Diane managed to shake her head.

"We're just as impermanent as anybody else. Everyone suffers. Think about all the other people with sick children, not whether you can stand it or not."

Lama S. swept out, leaving everyone quivering in her wake.

Lynn found a new doctor who was at least willing to talk to her. But he offered little beside sympathy. The situation was complicated because of lack of money. Julie's father had gone off to a Grateful Dead concert five years before and hadn't been heard from since. Lynn and Julie lived for free at Dorje Ling as Lynn worked as baker and kitchen gofer. In addition, she was one of the few women on the construction crew and, they all said, the best drywaller in the bunch. For pin money, she built and sold a few *puja* benches through the store, but mainly she and Julie just got along without much of anything. The past Christmas, Lynn had taken Julie down to Redding to the dollar store and told her she could have anything in the whole store that she wanted.

"Anything?" Julie's eyes had gone round at the very thought. Lynn said it had taken Julie an hour and a half to pick out a dishtowel set, which Lynn found in her own stocking on Christmas morning.

Now Lynn was completely dependent on state agencies, filling out form after form. The members of the *sangha* helped out where they could. Everyone bought a *puja* bench, but when Lynn's stock ran out, she didn't have time to make any more. Finally, the kitchen began to sell bread and muffins through a natural foods store in town, giving the proceeds to Lynn and Julie. It wasn't enough, but at least it was something we could do.

The lamas prayed, shook their heads, prayed again. After an especially bad seizure, Lama Tashi stayed up all night holding Julie in his arms, chanting. But nothing helped.

Three months later, when I entered the intensive care unit of the Oakland Children's Hospital, I thought I'd encountered a hell realm. The noise and harsh lights hit me like a barrage of field artillery. I could hear several people crying, a burn patient screaming, someone else arguing, another person begging the nurse for attention. A deep-voiced preacher prayed over a restless little boy while his mother cried and cried. Nurses trotted quickly by, one carrying a foul-smelling basin. Monitors bleeped and blared.

I finally found Lynn sitting with her head down on Julie's bed. Part of Julie's head had been shaved; she looked like a big-eyed alien. She didn't seem to recognize me.

"Lynn?"

When Lynn raised her head, I could see that she'd been crying hard. Her eyes were so puffy they were almost shut, her face red and blotchy. Nothing macho about Lynn now. I went over and took her hand, crouching down beside her since there was no other chair. The preacher started in our direction, but we immediately waved him away.

"I came as soon as I heard." The phone call had come from Lonny, who'd gone down to the hospital with Lynn and Julie. They'd finally arranged for Julie to have a complete workup at the Children's Hospital, get her medication right once and for all.

But it hadn't turned out that way. The tests showed that Julie had a brain tumor. A fast-growing malignant tumor that was causing all of the seizures. It had never been epilepsy. The baseball injury was simply a red herring, not related. There was nothing that could be done. And not much time left.

The burn patient screamed again, a long horrible cry.

Julie's eyes met mine, pleading.

"We've got to get you out of here, Sweet Pea. Spring you from this joint."

Julie smiled ever so slightly and closed her eyes.

"I don't know how to do this," Lynn told me about a month later. "I don't know what I'm supposed to do."

"Neither do I." I sat on a bench at the foot of Julie's bed. Lynn had just woken up and Julie still slept. The week before, the two of them had moved from their cabin at the top of the hill to the main Dorje Ling guest bedroom to make the round-the-clock watch on Julie easier. It was a large, airy room with a balcony overlooking the row of eight *stupas,* the mountains bluish in the distance.

I was always there when Lynn first woke up.

"I'm so glad that you take the early shift," she told me. "So I can fart when I wake up."

"Poot away, Lynn-la. Feel free." Every morning, I would come in at six, watch Lynn's sleeping face, relaxed, happy, soft. Then watch her wake, remember, quickly check to see if Julie was still breathing. Lynn's face by then a study of pain and worry.

A knock at the door. "Who's there?"

"It's me, Tulku Turd." He gave us a wicked grin before he sat down beside Julie on the bed and took her hand. She moved closer to him, her body just a slight blip under the covers. He just sat there, holding her hand. Brushed and washed, his fourth-grade homework sticking out of his jacket pocket, he simply sat and was still. I wondered how he'd learned that stillness.

Julie herself grew peaceful when he was in the room, seemed to respond to him as she did to no one else. Soon, he made it a habit to come to sit with her every morning before he went to school, since he had soccer practice in the afternoons. "It's TT the Little Shit," he'd call through the door before coming in.

Julie grew worse.

"There's some dark red material in the back of my car," Lynn told me. "I need . . ." she started crying. "I can't do it."

"Ah." I knew she wanted a robe ready for Julie.

I took the heavy red cotton back to the sewing room that night. As I made each careful stitch, I prayed for Julie's safe passage. In the neckline, I embroidered a tiny endless knot, then added a string of lotus flowers on the sash. Remembering the Jizo ceremony, I prayed to the *bodhisattva,* asking him to guide and protect the little girl. Then I prayed to Jesus. To God. To whomever was out there.

I also prayed for Lynn. I suspected that at this point Lynn probably needed more help than Julie. A few days before, the sickroom had been crowded with people in a frenzy of trying to help. They'd brought flowers, books, toys, statues of the Buddha. They came with useless bits of advice: shark cartilage was mentioned as a possible treatment; psychic healers in the Philippines should be consulted. Everyone wanted to *do* something

Before I left that day, I asked Julie if she needed anything.

"I'm fine," Julie, who had not talked in days, told me. "Just fine."

"Well, you're about the only one around here who is," I said as I kissed her goodbye. "We just don't know what to do. None of us."

Only Tulku Purba and the lamas were able to sit next to Julie, steady and still.

"She's in pain. She needs to go. Wants to." Lama P. was talking quietly to Lynn. The Tibetans taught that if people by a deathbed cried and carried on, it disturbed the smooth passage of the dying person. Everyone at Dorje Ling had tried to keep their own grief and fear outside of

Julie's room, even Lynn. But it hadn't always been possible. "The lamas think that she won't be able to go if you are in the room."

Silence. Sobbing.

"Maybe you can help with lunch."

It had been awful for the past week. Julie had started making a *nnnnyyyy* sound, throwing her head from side to side. She no longer ate, only took a little water from a dropper. Then she'd started to poop again. Great masses of shit. We all knew the time had come. Lynn hadn't left the room in days.

I held out my hand to Lynn and led her from the room.

We cooked in silence. As I browned the eggplant for moussaka, Lynn, face blank, began the dolmas. She dipped the grape leaves in boiling water, leaving them in the colander to drain while she made the stuffing. Concentrating hard, she browned the minced lamb with onions, then added rice and parsley. Every move she made was deliberate, concentrated. She moved around the kitchen with precision, like a dancer learning new steps. Rolling up the dolmas, she took care that not a single grain of rice escaped, that no edges gaped. Each one was tied exactly with a bit of string, their lengths evenly trimmed. When she'd used up the entire package of grape leaves, when the dolmas were neatly lined up in their baking trays, she went on to the next task.

It felt to me as if the kitchen itself was holding its breath, waiting along with us. Everything seemed white and blank. I could hear the lamas and staff start to assemble in the shrine room to be ready to say the prayers for the dead. Lynn did not look toward the door or even glance up from the phyllo pastry she was covering with butter for the spinach pie.

Dipping her fingers in the butter, she smoothed it onto the pastry sheets with infinite care, her attention narrowed to the dough, making sure that each millimeter was evenly covered. Then she'd coat the next sheet, and the next. Her face empty, blank, unearthly.

I didn't know how long we had been in the kitchen. I couldn't remember anything before, couldn't envision anything after. Just this blankness stretching on and on as the Greek food around us piled up. Enough to feed a small village. But still we kept making more, heaping up platters of pilaf, *tiropita,* baklava.

Just after noon, Lonny came into the kitchen, biting her lip. Julie was gone.

PART TWO

Don't Expect Applause

THIRTEEN

Restaurant Voices

LONG BEFORE I came to Dorje Ling, when I was still teaching at the university, I wrote a lot about the various kitchens I'd trained in. I had learned not only about food service, but also how to focus in the midst of change, how to surf the moment. Since impermanence rules the kitchen and all the processes therein, in Buddhist terms, it provides an ideal training ground for what is called View.

View means that we see the context of our experience in terms of emptiness, not in the sense of nothingness, but empty of our ideas about it. One of our main fixed ideas is that the world is solid and permanent, but this is not the case. The world is coming into being and going out of being simultaneously, like writing on water. The world is flowing, and we can learn to surf that movement.

Training in View entails—among other things—having someone home, someone responsible for the actions and activity of body, speech, and mind. In View itself, we are spontaneously present, accepting whatever comes along, as it happens, with no projections from the self formerly known as "I."

In addition, within the context of View, the self is

deconstructed and the seeming solidity of a sense of "I" fades, fails, dissolves into light and movement.

One of the techniques for establishing View is simply to see what you see or listen to sounds without putting them into any sort of framework, that is, not tripping out on them, not responding to them with attachment or aversion, not following thoughts about them. When I started writing about the restaurant I'd worked in, I realized that one of the pleasures there had been listening to the sounds from the dining room. That cacophony fed us in the kitchen, added the juice we needed to make it through the rest of the night.

Now I see that the training in the real-time world of restaurant kitchens helped prepare me for life with the always surprising Tibetans, as well as the pressure-cooker conditions found in a Dharma center.

Restaurant work isn't for sissies, nor is Tibetan Buddhism.

Lama P. says that doing spiritual work, training as a *bodhisattva,* takes a certain kind courage. A *bodhisattva,* by the way, is a person who is trying to align his or her mind with the path of the buddhas in order to be happier and more effective in dealing with others.

In trying to get the mind under control, the *bodhisattva* works with the five poisons of anger, attachment, ignorance, jealousy, and pride in order to transform them to the five wisdoms.

In terms of conduct, the *bodhisattva*-in-training studies the six perfections: generosity, patience, diligence, moral discipline, concentration, and wisdom. When we apply emptiness to the first five perfections, this becomes the sixth, wisdom. I found that the kitchen, almost any kitchen, provided the perfect boot camp for developing the six perfections. The heat and the speed there demands that we live in real time, always on the edge of control and without our usual defenses. In short, it's hard to pretend patience when your hair is on fire. Either patience comes up spontaneously or it doesn't show. If not, then we're told to look for where and why we lost it. When we find that little spot at the edge of the mind, we try to rest there for a while, asking, Who is it that is so impatient?

Part of the training is to bring the mind back to View again and again. That means not stopping and saying, "Oy vey, forgive me, I lost it" or tripping out about it in any way. Simply return to View and keep going.

The gaps between holding View range from a nano-second to a lifetime. Part of the training in stability is to herd your thoughts into View mode until it becomes automatic. Lama P. says this gets easier with practice.

When it becomes automatic, then you can rest in the nature of your mind in a natural, uncontrived way. This is called *rigpa*. One of the purposes of the training is to learn to maintain this state not only on the cushion, but off the cushion and in dreams. When circumstances and karmic events erupt that make you lose View, prayer helps, as does guru yoga.

This is some of the spiritual work of the person who wishes to train in the path of the buddhas. According to Lama P., to be actively engaged in the process of applying the six perfections, of holding View, and so on, makes you a practitioner. He said that not everyone who lived at Dorje Ling was a practitioner, although they all had their moments.

FOURTEEN

My Short but Violent Career As a Chef

"WHERE DID YOU GO to chef school?" Maya, from Portland, asked me one day. She wanted to become a chef, the fool.

"Just trained on the job."

"How does that work?"

"It means that you do the dirty work for as long as you are willing to be underpaid. When you ask for more money or better conditions, you are trained."

"But . . ." she started, then thought better of it. "So you just went to a restaurant and said, 'I want to be a chef,' and they taught you to cook?"

"Actually, I started out in a pizza parlor."

"You did? Really? How did that happen?"

"Divorce. He and I were teaching in the same department and it made everyone uncomfortable, so I thought I'd try to get a job somewhere else." I had skipped over a small mountain of messy details. The truth was that divorce had plunged me into poverty from one day to the next. I'd been a graduate student at the time, he a tenured faculty member. I'd grown sick to tears of the university, all it stood for and the people in it. All in their heads, I ranted, fumed. So when I left my husband, I somehow couldn't make myself apply for any more teaching jobs that year either. Then I ran out of money, never having thought to stash any away for an unmarried state. And there I was in that pizza parlor.

"The mushrooms go on top, otherwise the pizza gets watery. This is Mike." The manager of the restaurant pointed to an evil-looking adolescent glowering by the sink. "The two of you work together back here." The manager put wads of dough through a sort of wringer, which pressed out flat circles for crust. I wanted to touch the machine, wanted him to leave so I could handle the big pans and two-foot-long spoons, but he kept on talking.

"The waitress puts the orders up here," he said, indicating a sort of clothesline. "You make the pizza like the order says: BO is black olives, P is pepperoni, and so on. Look at the menu. Ask Mike if you got questions."

Suddenly he was gone, the swinging door flapping. Mike pursed his lips like a fish about to feed, scratched his groin, and lurched outside, leaving me alone in the pizza pie department of the restaurant kitchen.

"Assistant to the Chef" is what the ad had said. Different from Assistant Chef, which took a longer time, more training. I was to start by "getting to know the restaurant operation." Code for "at the bottom." Tonight I would make pizza pies, but I was to be trained as a chef.

A real chef. I fingered the white apron reverently and

started to slice up, no, *prep* the vegetables that would top the pizzas, heaping them in a rack of stainless steel containers at the back of the work table.

When, separated from my husband, I started combing the want ads for a "suitable" job, I'd found such possibilities as Assistant Museum Curator, Manager Trainee, Executive Secretary. All required subservience, respectability, panty hose. Then I saw the ad for Assistant to the Chef and felt my inner landscape pause, shift. A chef? Why not? I loved food, loved to cook, to eat. Felt happiest when working in a kitchen. During the years I'd spent teaching English, everything had become words, and words about words. The parties Richard and I hosted were famous throughout the department, if not all of Arts and Sciences. But to be able to create an intricate meal and then not to have to sit down and eat with the guests? That was a pleasure I had never even imagined.

Instinct told me to hide my various advanced degrees from the manager of the restaurant. I didn't claim to have an education at all, nope, not me. The restaurant, famous for its pizza and beer, also served Italian entrées, so I'd boned up on *spezzatino di pollo* and *gnocchi di patate.* I wanted to tell him that gnocchi must be added singly to the boiling water, that overcrowding . . . but all he'd asked was what time I could come in the next day.

A teenager with purple lipstick and a short shirt appeared from the dining room. "Where's Mike?"

"Mike? I think he went out back." Must be the waitress. Was it that close to dinner?

"God. Another one," I heard her say to Mike. What did she mean by that? Another what? Another employee? Another . . . The manager appeared.

"Marlene here yet?"

"Out back with Mike."

"What're they doing out there?" He looked at me as if I might know, but before I could say a word they both trooped in looking a bit fuzzy.

More introductions, explanations. Marlene gave me a gummy smile and as long as the manager stayed in sight seemed pleasant enough. The minute he left, she showed her teeth.

"You mess up and I'm the one that don't get a tip. Understand?"

"Doesn't." I corrected automatically, having taught English most of my adult life.

The speed and energy of the restaurant began to pick up, making me move faster and faster as I finished prepping the vegetables. The heaps were no longer neat: onions spilled over into green peppers, mushrooms edged over toward the olives. A charge, a we're-almost-ready-to-open charge felt good, exciting, alive.

For about five minutes. Then we opened. Customers came rushing through the door, demanding pizza, beer, service: everything harried, rushed, desperate. Waitresses bumped into each other, workers collided, plates and glasses went spinning. What had appeared to be infinite time in which to carefully cut up vegetables became compressed, then snatched away. On the empty line appeared six orders. SIX. None of which I could read, nor could I get Marlene's attention long enough to ask her to explain.

It had sounded fairly easy: I mean, what's it to make a pizza? The sauce, prepared in a separate kitchen across the street, arrived in large buckets, had to be measured out on the dough, then the toppings put on. Simple. Easy as pizza pie.

Yes, but only if you do one at a time. When there are six to be made and sliced and served at once, when bread sticks have to be rolled and baked and the pans for all of these washed and put back into use, it gets more complicated. Not impossible, just complicated. Working at the speed of heat, I managed to get the first round of pizzas in the oven, but the silly waitress kept waiting on people, so I had barely closed the oven door when a whole new string of orders came in.

Goddamn, I complained to myself, this is hard. I mean hard. Fortunately, the manager arrived and told Mike to take over getting the pizzas out of the oven, that they were behind. He didn't smile at me this time, just scowled at the orders above my prep table. But I hadn't stopped a single minute, not even one. My attention narrowed to the prep table—dough, sauce, black olives, cheese; dough, sauce, onions and green peppers, cheese. I liked the feeling of attention being tightly focused on something besides the written word. I'd talked a lot about trying to get beyond language, trying to let go. And here . . . but I didn't even finish the thought. Dough, sauce, Italian sausage, green pepper, onions, cheese, extra cheese, dough, sauce, pepperoni, cheese, dough . . . "What?" Why was Marlene so furious?

"I asked for onions and bacon. You gimme olives."

I checked the order and held it in Marlene's distorted face. "BO. BO stands for black olives. That's what the manager said and that's what I gave you."

"BO stands for bacon and onions. Always has. Always will."

"But . . ." I talked to the air since Marlene had flounced out. "Shit."

One more to add to the orders. Dough, sauce . . . but the big sauce bucket sat empty. How could I make pizzas without sauce? "Mike. Mike? I'm out of sauce."

"Tough shit." He didn't even turn around to say it.

"Well, what do I do now?"

Silence.

"I'm completely out of sauce."

"Guess you better find some more."

"But there're about a dozen orders here."

"Hand me that cutter, will you? Gotta slice this here pizza."

Then his back again. Stunned, I picked up the bucket, stood undecided for a moment. So this is how it is when people aren't surrounded by rules, committees, university ombudsmen.

I started out the door and across the street to the alternate kitchen. The fresh air felt wonderful. I'd forgotten. Open spaces, light, air. How long had it been? Weeks? Months? The world surprised me by continuing at a normal rate of speed. People were walking by. Walking, not running, not hurtling things. Unconcerned, relaxed, talking to each other in a pleasant way. Not screaming, not swearing, just talking. I sighed deeply and went into the alternate kitchen.

No one seemed to be there, so I pushed open the swinging door that led to the rear. Someone pushed back. Someone angry, shouting, telling me to leave.

"I'm the assistant chef and I need more sauce."

"Assistant chef here an hour ago and he ain't you."

"I mean the assistant to the chef. Anyway, I've run out of sauce for the pizza."

"Assistant to the chef? That's a new one. You on the pizza line? Five whole gallons of sauce in the cold room over in the restaurant. Why didn't you get it outta there? You on break or what?"

"Cold room?"

"Right next to where you make the pizza."

"Shit."

"Sorry I yelled at you, lady, but don't nobody supposed to come in here. It's the rules."

Then a sound from the back took him away with a curse.

As I crossed the street, I could see the manager straining out the door, looking for me. *Angry* could be used to describe his state, but it is such an inadequate little word. *Angry* doesn't denote a condition of combined bodily tension, exhaustion, and despair. *Angry* doesn't imply being stared at by about twenty hungry customers.

Dodging cars, unable to explain at that distance, I held the bucket up, trying to make him understand my errand.

"Don't say anything," he hissed at me. "Just get to work."

"I ran out of sauce," I began, then nearly tripped over a bucketful placed by my work station.

"Saw you was running low, so I got you out some more sauce out of the cold room while you was taking your break." Mike, that devil, smiled innocently at me and batted his eyes at the manager.

"Oh," I began inadequately.

"We'll straighten this out later," claimed the manager, "but get going now." In the months to come I learned that later never came in the restaurant world. Never. But at that point, I turned back to the prep table only to be interrupted by Marlene.

"Where's all my pizzas? People out there are getting hungry. And mad. What am I supposed to tell them?"

Eat shit and die came to my mind, but Marlene had already snatched up my order and gone. I spun around to Mike, only to see his back: this time disappearing out the door.

Mike had a sort of genius for looking busy and doing nothing whatsoever. He spent most of the time out in the alley smoking dope, coming into the kitchen only to feed, certainly not to work. What he couldn't devour on the spot, he put near his jacket to take home and eat later.

Dough, sauce, bacon and onion, cheese; dough, sauce, mushrooms, cheese; dough, sauce, anchovies, cheese, extra cheese; dough, sauce . . . the smell of burning. A pan of Mike's bread sticks were smoking in the huge oven. Knowing I would somehow be blamed, I dumped out the blackened sticks and threw the mammoth flat sheet in the tub of the sink. I'd barely gotten back to my pile of orders when I heard a loud yell from Mike. Doubled over by the sink, clutching his hand, he cried piteously: "Ow. Ow. Ow." Then he began in a dull whine, "Look what you done to me. Shoulda called 'hot.' Shouldn't go around hurting people like that. You gotta call 'hot,' gotta be careful of them pans."

"Nobody ever said anything about calling 'hot.' Here, let me see the burn."

"Get away, bitch. Don't you touch me. Now I can't take my pizzas out of the oven. You got to take them out. Can't put these poor, blistered hands in water, neither. You got to wash them pans." Mike pointed to a small waste dump of assorted pans.

"Not 'them' pans. 'Those.'"

"All of them. Shoulda called 'hot.'"

Marlene stormed in. "Now you've done it again. I ordered a nine-inch pizza and you gimme a seven. Another table, mad as shit."

I looked at the order. "This says seven. Nine is the number that has the little loop up on top."

"Four people at the table don't order no seven."

"Well, I can't see the table. I can't see anything but the order and the fucking order says seven so I gave you a seven." I slammed the pizza dough onto the table and finished making the pizza almost before Marlene left the kitchen.

I'd learned one thing, anyhow: rage provides the energy for the kitchen. Rage is the power that keeps everyone moving, keeps hands heaping up food, keeps bodies upright and feet moving. Pure rage empowered me, made me catch up on the pizza orders, snatch them from the oven, sling them onto the table. A driving rage fed me as I slashed them into pieces, slammed them onto the serving port.

I didn't think again until hours later. Or rather I didn't have any consciousness of myself as a thinking being. Immersed in action, I felt like an athlete: the competition, the violence, the desire to win. Later the reaction set in—the sore muscles, the exhaustion—but at the time, I lived, quite literally, in the moment.

"Last order," Marlene announced.

Last order? Does that mean it stops? I looked at the clock: ten-thirty. Suddenly drained, I sat with a thump, a massive blankness settling over me.

The manager. "Why don't you get something to eat before you start to clean up." Clean up? Whatever did he mean? I ignored the implications and lurched toward the small kitchen where they made the entrées. The idea of eating pizza seemed utterly ridiculous.

A big, black stove with red knobs took up half the room. A wooden prep table covered with remains of dinners past stood under a hanging fluorescent fixture. Gigantic pots and pans hung here and there. Two men, both in chef's hats, looked up when I came in.

"Ah, the new girl from the pizza line. You hungry?"

Girl? Pizza line? They offered me spaghetti, ravioli, chicken cacciatore, minestrone, but suddenly I didn't want to eat. In fact, I said to them, I had mainly come in to introduce myself since I was, thank God, not really on the pizza line but had been hired as the assistant to the chef. The sooner I could start training in this kitchen the better.

A long, uncomfortable silence followed. They continued to offer me spaghetti and ravioli but were clearly embarrassed. Gradually it became clear that one of the men, a fat-assed Belgian, was the new assistant chef and neither had ever heard of the position of an assistant *to* the chef. Their kitchen, they assured me, was strictly a two-man operation. And going to stay that way.

So the manager had used the title just to lure me into making pizzas. He'd already filled the chef's position by the time I applied for it. Did he think I wouldn't notice? Or was it just that he didn't care? Just that he had to have someone on the pizza line that day.

When I got back, nothing had changed: an olive oil slick still covered a large area near the door, pans teetered precariously on top of pans in and around the sink, bits of vegetables and cheese still littered the work table and the floor. Mike was nowhere to be seen.

But the manager stood there with a mop in his hand. "After this gets scrubbed up, you'll have to mop." He did have the decency to look away. "Dangerous with all that oil there."

"Mop?" I had been on my feet eight hours, cooped up with an escapee from an S/M cult, subjected to manipulation, rejection, humiliation, and he wanted me to mop the floor? Near midnight? To mop that which should be shoveled out and hosed down by two large, fresh men? I could barely stand and he wanted me to put a mop in water and slosh it around on the floor?

"Yes, mop."

Mike appeared from the back. "I can't mop," he whined. "Made me burn myself. Didn't call 'hot.' "

"Floor gets mopped at the end of the shift," the manager announced decisively.

"Listen," I said, using the tone of voice I'd adopted with students who'd missed too many classes. "I want to talk to you."

"Sure. I'll be out in the dining room. Come on out when you've finished cleaning up in here."

I found myself holding the mop, staring at the swinging door, the breath of cool air it let through creating a memory of freedom, the hint of another, better world.

I hung, undecided, until I saw a smile spreading across Mike's face like a rapidly growing cancer. He slouched forward, tilted his pelvis in my direction. Unclasping his hand, he drew a pack of cigarettes from his pocket, opening them with hands able to move, able to flick the lighter without flinching, to hold the flame steadily in front of his cupped palms.

He hadn't been burned at all, the lying bastard.

Well, at least I have restaurant experience now, I told myself as I set the mop against the sink and slipped quietly out the back door, barely glancing at Mike. Not that I care, I added, as I began to sniff gratefully at the cool night air, a long-penned animal, suddenly released.

"So then what happened?" Maya asked the next time we cooked together. "After you quit the pizza parlor."

"I started working in a small, downtown restaurant owned by these two crazy brothers. One of them was the chef I trained under."

I could have stopped after my one and only night at the pizza parlor. Maybe found a job as an editor or journalist. But I didn't. The idea of becoming a chef had taken hold of me despite the fact that I could barely move the next morning. I felt minced, boned, pureed, reduced by half. But something had drawn me toward the restaurant world—or perhaps just pushed me away from where I'd been. At any rate, I walked into yet another restaurant a few days later.

"Lots of experience," I told the man in front of me. "Pizza place when I was younger. Catering . . ." I let my voice trail off, trying to suggest that I simply had too much background to try to talk about it all.

"Who were you catering for?"

"Richard's Parties."

"Never heard of them."

"Did lots of parties out at the university."

We stood in the muted blue-gray hush of the dining room of Lafayette's, a fairly new restaurant in the historic district of town. Several small rooms opened into each other, creating a sense of both privacy and spaciousness. Walls, carpets, upholstery, and linen were done in various soft shades of blue and gray, while at the windows hung heavy blue velvet draperies, edged and pulled back with thick gold braid. The white lace inner curtains across the lower half of the windows screened the room from the street while letting in filtered light. Two of the rooms had carved marble mantelpieces, one topped with white roses in a Wedgwood vase.

"They ate here," the man was saying, as if I'd asked. "Henry Clay and General Lafayette. The building was Clay's law office then, but since miraculously it never got put on the Historic Register, my brother and I were able to convert it. Been in the family for ages, of course, just sitting here. I mean, who wants to live downtown? Anyway, two years ago, when Julian came back from France, we decided to turn it into a restaurant for him."

"Your brother is the chef?"

"An absolute genius with food. Jules could always cook, but after France—ooh, la, la." His hand fluttered upward.

"He trained there?"

"Yes, indeed."

"Where, exactly? I know someone who . . ." But before I could finish, Whitney Clay Sloan III had turned away to tsk over a tiny spot on a tablecloth. He had introduced himself just that way—Whitney Clay Sloan III—without telling me what to call him. He seemed about forty-five, soft around the middle, balding on top with longish wisps of fine brown hair over the collar of his pale yellow silk shirt. The three last names were the tip-off, but he also had that self-contained, somewhat distracted look that often comes with old money.

"We had no idea that this color would show spots so badly." He looked sorrowfully at the tablecloth.

"Has the restaurant been open long?"

"Only six months. The renovation of the building took ages. Then the decoration." Again the upward flutter of the hand.

"It always seems to take forever, doesn't it? But it's lovely." And it was. The rooms didn't have a decorated look at all, nor that shiny polish of newness. Everything fit together in understated elegance.

Whitney Clay Sloan III gazed around in satisfaction, letting his eye linger on each carefully chosen detail. He seemed to have forgotten that I was there to interview for a job as a sous-chef. "The colors *are* lovely, aren't they? We were afraid that the Wedgwood blue might be a little cold, but I don't think so. Do you?"

"Oh, no."

He began stroking the velvet curtain, lost in contemplation. Maybe he thought that I'd just dropped in for a visit.

"The kitchen?" I prompted. "Did you redo the kitchen, too?"

Whitney Clay Sloan III sighed deeply and gave me a weary look. "Oh. The kitchen. Jules is in charge of all that. I suppose you'd better meet him."

He didn't move or stop stroking the velvet, but he did begin to tell me about the menu. "We're looking for someone who can help out mainly at lunch. We only serve a light lunch. Lots of salads. It seems that's what people like these days. We also do pâté boards, cheese plates, fruit assortments. That sort of thing. Customers from the neighborhood office buildings beg us for sandwiches, but so far we've held out."

"Held out?"

"Well, we're not just some common *joint* after all."

"Oh."

"We're Lafayette's. Top of the line."

"Hm."

"No sandwiches. No Cokes. No potato chips."

"Ah."

"Nice soups, salads, light lunches. Dinner, of course, there we go way out."

"Of course."

He drifted off again.

"And your brother does the dinners?"

He sighed more deeply than before and motioned for me to follow him down a long, dark passage. The sense of finely wrought harmony ended abruptly, giving way to the feeling of being in an old, run-down house. Closets and small storerooms spilled their contents out into the hall. Brooms, mops, linens, stacks of canned goods, fifty-pound mesh bags of onions and potatoes jumbled together. The passage ended in a small room where it seemed restaurant equipment was being stored. I realized that we were in the kitchen, and that we were not alone.

"Julian, this young lady is here about the job."

The boy standing by the prep table seemed much too young to be the other man's brother. Nor did they look anything alike. The cigarette-thin person called Julian had large, startled brown eyes and a fey air that made it seem he was on the verge of disappearing. We waited in silence as he continued to concentrate on chopping green peppers.

"Julian, I spoke to you," Whitney Clay Sloan III said sternly. He sounded like a father or stepfather. "Julian!"

Julian still didn't look up.

"JULES!"

"Yes?" he said sweetly, as innocent as a baby waking from a nap.

His brother's face flushed a deep, angry red, and he stood breathing hard, clenching and unclenching his fists. Julian gave me a beatific smile, then went on chopping peppers.

"Hi," I said tentatively.

"You're a chef?" He put his head to one side, then the other, peering at me.

"Yes," I lied.

"Can you cook?" His voice was sweet and clear like a child's.

"Oh, yes." I *could* cook.

"You don't look like a chef. You're very pretty."

"Thank you." I wanted to add, "So are you" but didn't. But that was just the word for him: a cloud of blond ringlets framed his delicate face, setting off his large eyes, Cupid's-bow mouth, and high coloring. "You don't look like a chef either."

"I guess they're usually bigger. I'm five foot five. How tall are you?"

"Five foot four."

"That's a good height. Rocky is almost six feet."

"Rocky?"

"The luncheon chef. You'll be working with her."

Whitney Clay Sloan III began to make noises which Julian ignored.

"She needs help during lunch, and then I need someone to prep for me in the afternoons. Tony comes in around five-thirty or six and helps me serve dinner."

"What Jules means to say is that whomever we hire will be doing this," his brother interrupted. "Mother and I had decided we should hire a man, so if you . . ."

"Can you work from nine to about four or five, weekdays?"

"Sure." I didn't take my eyes off Julian, although I could see his brother waving his arms.

"You'll have to start at minimum wage, but then if you work out, the salary will go up."

"Really, Jules, you don't have the right to do this."

"You're not a Capricorn, are you?" Jules asked.

I shook my head. "Scorpio." Both sun and moon in Scorpio, actually, but I didn't want to scare him.

"Great, I always get along with Scorpio women."

"What are you?"

"What do you think?"

"Hmm. Maybe a . . . Pisces?" I don't know why I said that since I didn't know much at all about astrology, but—to Jules's glee—I'd guessed right.

"What's your rising sign?"

"Honestly, Jules, you haven't the slightest idea how to conduct an interview. We're looking for someone with very specific skills. Someone who . . ."

Jules ignored his brother. "You'll have to go to the Health Department and get a permit from them. Unless you already have one?"

"No, I don't."

"You aren't really a chef, are you?" Jules's voice was mild, friendly, curious.

"Not yet."

He gave me a big smile. "Good. What are you, then?"

"A former wife. A recovering academic. But I *can* cook."

He laughed in delight while his brother The Third looked at me in horror.

"I taught at the university. Actually, I'm still supposed to have a job there. But this man—well, he's sort of my husband—he's in the same department." I skipped over a small mound of messy details, including the fact that the department secretary had warned me that all I was going to get to teach from then on was bonehead English. "It got awkward," I concluded with a shrug.

"What did you teach?"

"Women's studies. Poetry and creative writing when I got the chance."

"I used to write poetry," Jules told me.

"Used to?"

"I haven't in ages. No time."

I was about to ask Julian to bring in some of his poetry for me to look at when he said, "You're perfect. Come in tomorrow around nine."

Whitney Clay Sloan III made little snorting sounds, but I pretended not to notice as I left the kitchen. Walking down the passage, I could hear him say, "Perfect, indeed. Another untrained person! Mother isn't going to put up with this. Not this time. You won't be able to twist her around your little finger, Julian, like you did when you hired Rocky. And why you ever hired *her* is still beyond human comprehension."

He was still talking as I walked out into the blue-gray cocoon of the dining room.

The next day, life as I had always known it stopped, halted dead in its tracks at the restaurant door. In its place lay a world that went at a different speed, operated by a separate and desperate set of laws. This world of heat and pressure always seemed on the verge of explosion, always a threat to those within.

Lafayette's had two major shifts: lunch and dinner, with a chef and a helper for each. In terms of mechanics, lunch was by far harder, since they served more people more quickly and had to have the kitchen cleaned up before the dinner crew could begin. After lunch, Jules and I would work together until late afternoon, when his sous-chef, Tony, would come in and help him during dinner. Since I had been hired as kitchen help, I held the very lowest position in the feeding chain. Every dirty job eventually got passed on to me.

Whitney Clay Sloan III—before he disappeared for the day—gave me over to Rocky, the luncheon chef, a huge woman with tattooed arms, and asked her to "break me in." An unfortunate phrase.

A mountain of a woman, Rocky was dressed in jeans, a man's flannel shirt, and a red Cardinals baseball cap turned backward over dark, stringy hair. A little near-sighted, she had a habit of sticking out her neck and peering intently at a thing. Or at a person, who soon began to feel like a thing.

"You stay on that side of the kitchen while you make the salads," she said, pointing to a long work table with refrigeration underneath and stainless steel wells toward the back. "Slice up the veggies and put them in here, 'shrooms here, shredded lettuce there, 'maters here." She jabbed at the metal containers as she pointed, making them rattle in their wells. She leaned closer to me and began to whisper. "We also does sandwiches."

"What?" I whispered back. "Sandwiches?"

"Whit don't know."

"You mean Whitney Clay so forth?"

"Who else? Now, he's real particular about the menu. He don't like the idea of Lafayette's selling sandwiches. But we likes to give people what they want."

She reared back as if this explained everything.

"So?"

"So we don't put them on the menu!"

"But . . . ? People can order them anyway? Under the counter?"

"Just the regulars. And only on days when Whit ain't here."

"I see. I guess."

"He goes in spurts."

"Spurts?"

"Working spurts. You'll see. But I keep things going when he ain't around. Jules is the one what hired me."

"Does Jules know about the sandwiches?"

"Shhh. He don't care nothing about lunch. Just dinner. I'm trying to help them make money. Don't have much sense, neither of them boys. My ma used to work for Jules's pa. Says he didn't have much sense neither. Now. Where was we? Oh. Here. The waiter puts the orders up on this here wheel, when it's done, you take the ticket with the order and put it in there." She pointed to a clumsy-looking shelf that acted as a serving port. "When you put up an order, you ding the bell." She banged on the bell to show me how it worked. "You can't hear it in the dining room lest you ding it real loud.

"This here is the prep table. I do the main dishes and the soups over here." She jerked a thumb at "her" side of the kitchen where the big stove hulked. The prep table marked the boundary between the two territories, a boundary never violated by either shift except in the most extreme emergencies—shooting flames, gushing water, et cetera. "We do two soups at lunch and three entries. They'll start coming in soon, the lunch crowd. Better be ready.

"This here's the sink." I dutifully looked where Rocky pointed. Yep, that there sure was the sink, all right. "Dirty dishes go in the first tub, you wash them there in the middle tub and rinse them in this here third tub. Put a tablet of disinfectant in the rinse water." She held up a box of blue tablets. "Then put the rinsed dishes here on the drying rack." She glared and leaned toward me. "You do the dishes after lunch and clean up the kitchen."

Whit had told me that Rocky and I would share the cleanup, but clearly it wasn't going to work out that way.

"I do the entries and the soups over here." She indicated her side of the kitchen again. "We do two soups at lunch and three entries."

"Entrées," I couldn't help saying. "Not 'entries.'"

Fortunately, Rocky didn't hear, but had lumbered over to the stove to warm up the cream for the white sauce. Rocky clearly found explaining things a great strain, as if she and language had never been on very good terms. Talking to her felt like dropping stones down a well.

After a few minutes, Rocky started to sweat, although the kitchen remained relatively cool. "Go get me some ice water," she suddenly ordered. "Out there." Indicating the bar.

Well, I thought, startled, at least I don't have to wear panty hose.

"She got a personality like a riptide or what?" The bartender held out a beer mug of water and ice to me, smiling.

"Like being in a hot tub with a water buffalo. Is she always like that?"

"Nyah. She's on her good behavior right now. Wait till lunch."

"Oh, dear."

"It'll start pretty soon, but the lunch crowd is fairly tame. All they really want is a quick sandwich and a Coke, no matter what Sir Whitney might think. Leave a quarter tip. Wait until tonight, when the regulars come in. Then you'll see some real action."

He wheeled cases of beer behind the bar and began putting them into the cooler.

"You got my water?" Rocky blared from the kitchen. I had forgotten her for a brief, blissful moment.

Rocky seemed to be sweating more profusely now. "Got to get this work done," she muttered. "Takes time to train people, time oughta go to cooking."

That was training? I sliced tomatoes and arranged an assembly line of little piles of meat and cheese and relishes. Rocky muttered in the background. "Got to cook the rice. Twenty-five minutes. Got to remember to order more lemon juice. We're running out of lemon juice. Got to get the soup on. Don't know what soup to have today. Getting late. Getting real late. Add to last night's soup." Mutter, mutter.

"You finish the work list?" Rocky asked me.

"Work list?"

"Yeah, the work list. You do what's on the work list?"

I had done everything Rocky had told me to do, so I figured that must be the work list. "Yeah."

"*This* list?" Rocky held up a grubby piece of paper.

I looked at the childish scrawl. "Yeah, I finished all that."

This seemed to irritate Rocky. In fact, everything about me seemed to irritate Rocky. "Don't cut those tomatoes so thick. Tomatoes cost money. Cut those slices in half."

The tomatoes slices weren't *that* thick. Was she joking? But one look at Rocky told me that she wasn't trying to be funny. "Well," I exclaimed under my breath, sounding just like my mother. "*Well!*"

The closer we came to lunch, the higher ran the tension in the kitchen. Rocky's movements became increasingly jerky, more and more out of control. Her water glass went skittering across the prep table onto my side of the kitchen. "Now look what you done!"

I stared at her in astonishment.

"I gotta get out of this shithole." Rocky charged out to the bar, "Gonna get me more ice."

"Listen, Whit," I heard her say from the bar. "Next time get trained help, okay? I've got enough to do without fooling around training somebody. She's gonna use up all the tomatoes in the first fifteen minutes. Then you'll have to go get more."

I could hear Whit offering soothing, murmuring sounds. I folded my arms in disgust and made an impatient noise until I realized—for the second time that morning—how much like my mother I sounded. I had spent a large part of my life trying not to be like my mother. ("Matraphobia," I would tell my women's studies class, "is not the fear of one's mother, as you might think, but the fear of *becoming* one's mother.") I had vivid memories of my mother standing at a dress store counter with arms folded, trying to get a gum-chewing clerk's attention by making little disgusted sounds. ("The Southern Lady," I had explained to the same class, "is a somewhat dangerous social type who bases her assumptions of personal privilege on her economic class, family lineage, and race. She does not question the patriarchal order of the South, but exploits it to her own ends of personal power and control. At present these women are somewhat an endangered species and will, hopefully, in time, disappear.")

I willed myself to unfold my arms, to breathe deeply and evenly. I hadn't come this far just to turn into my mother. Rocky huffed and puffed around the dining room, then poured straight vodka into her water glass and headed back into the kitchen.

Lunch itself was relatively easy. Fast paced, yes, but nothing I couldn't handle. The hardest part was to remember that when an order came in marked SALAD, it could mean either salad or sandwich, depending on whether Whit was in the dining room and whether the customer was a regular. Rocky, sure that Whit would go through the orders when he added up the receipts, only let the word *sandwich* be whispered. Finally, I worked out a system with the waiter, a lean, square-jawed young man named Z., in which he'd circle the word *salad* if it really meant sandwich. That way, I'd be able to tell at a glance, but Whit would never guess that someone's chicken salad had been put between two slices of bread instead of on lettuce with the bread served on a separate plate. They kept the contraband potato chips beneath the counter in a large container marked FLOUR.

After that, it was smooth sailing. At least on my side of the kitchen. Over by the stove, Rocky stamped and lunged, swore and snorted, clattered and banged, yelled and puffed, crashed and tore her way through lunch.

"Four soups, yes sirree, four soups coming up. No problem. No problem at all. Two coq au vin. Gettin' um, two coqs coming up. There you are two coqs. Now two more soups, cream soup this time, gots lots of cream soup, put them in bowls, put them on the shelf, ring the bell. COME GET YOUR SOUP WHILE IT'S HOT. Now what? Chicken livers, oh my god, two fucking chicken livers, get them suckers out of the cooler, put them in hot butter, DON'T SPIT AT ME, YOU LITTLE FUCKERS. Two soup gotta wait. Got to get these here chicken livers. Pour brandy on them. Light them. Oh, my God, flames shooting all over the place. HOLY SHIT. Gonna burn us up one of these days. I KNOW YOU WANT TWO SOUPS. YOU'LL GET THEM WHEN YOU GET THEM. Bed of rice. Put the little fuckers on a bed of rice. Ring the bell. COME GET YOUR FUCKING CHICKEN LIVERS. Two soups, got to dish up two soups." And so it went for almost three hours.

After lunch, immediately after lunch, Rocky threw down her apron, picked up the brandy bottle, and headed for the back porch, where she thunked down in an old easy chair. I finished dishing up the desserts and started to wash the small mountain of dishes that had collected. Actually, I found something soothing about working in hot water, something satisfying about stacking up clean dishes. Also, it was such a relief to be in the kitchen by myself that I didn't care about anything else.

The longer I worked at Lafayette's, the more the rest of the world began to slide into the background; outside people became flat and uninteresting. David the bartender showed me how he mixed drinks, how he put in the ice and mixer first, then the booze on top, so the drink seemed stronger. He taught me how to fan a stack of paper napkins into a neat spiral, how to play games with straws and matchbooks. His favorite trick was to poke holes in the covers of Pep Boys matches, then pull through three match stems so it looked like Manny, Moe, and Jack each had his own little red-tipped penis.

Certainly the academic world that I'd left behind seemed light years away. Here in the grubby kitchen, the intellectual posturing of literary criticism was hard to remember, even to imagine. Did grown-up people really spend hours arguing about what a character in a book written two centuries ago should or shouldn't have done? Or deconstruct a paragraph until the words were minced as finely as garlic for scampi?

I developed the habit of sitting on the end of the bar after my workday as the dining room filled up with people who came from the neighboring downtown offices, stopping by for a drink on their way home. Later in the evening, an altogether different crowd began to drift in. Every night after the last dinner had gone out at Lafayette's, the Japanese prints on the wall would be turned over. "Viewing Cherry Blossoms" would become "Two Men in a Bath." A tiny card, just enough of a sign to let you know you'd found the place you were seeking, went up in the bar window: DIKI'S. Word of mouth was the only advertisement.

I hadn't known about the existence of Diki's until after months at Lafayette's. I knew that there was a bar, but not that they called it Diki's and not what went on there. Sometimes I'd be the only woman in the room, other times the only straight person. But they didn't really notice me in my dirty apron coming up to the bar to ask for ice cubes or sitting talking to David. I'd become part of the staff, the family, the inner heart of the scene. And what a scene. I wrote my play based on it: *Dragon Soup & Other Intense Sensations,* produced in a restaurant in California. That was years before I moved to Dorje Ling, back when I was simply trying to survive day to day in the working world.

"Okay." Maya was determined to finish hearing my chefing story before she had to go back home. "So how was it you got to be a luncheon chef?"

"My first job there was what they called the sous-chef, but I was just kitchen help, really. Rocky was the luncheon chef."

"So did you get to cook anything you wanted?"

"Pretty much. It was a free-form sort of a restaurant. Into crisis, into drama, into wondering if there would even be a future, much less one that we could plan for. But that was later, after I became luncheon chef. As kitchen help I didn't have any say in anything."

It had been, in fact a very humbling experience to be the lowest person on the feeding chain. But valuable. As one of the Zen masters says, when you have been humiliated enough, you learn humility.

"How did you get promoted?"

"Well, it started on a busy Friday."

Z., the waiter, zipped in and out of the kitchen leaving a string of sound behind: "FOURSOUPSTWOCRABLOUIS ONERATATOUILLE."

"What'd he say, what'd he say?" Rocky shoved me aside, reaching for the tickets on the wheel. Normally, the waiter would call out an order when he put the ticket up so that the chef could start on it right away. But today he flashed by too quickly for the orders to make sense. We were already behind, and Rocky, as a therapist might have tactfully put it, was fast losing her coping skills.

"ONERATATOUILLEONECHEESEPLATENOSWISS."

Friday lunch: the weekend crowd started early, and the usual weekday customers had to fight for their ham sandwiches and Cokes. Most of the "weekend" Friday customers ordered entrées, and of course on that particular day, the restaurant would be a little low on everything. Nor was anything ready (except at my station), since Jules, Whit, and Rocky had spent the morning arguing about who was to be in charge of the new Saturday brunch. According to Whit, Rocky, as luncheon chef, should take the shift, since Jules had to do dinner. She, on the other hand, said that she wasn't about to start working on Saturday mornings in addition to being there all week. Jules had thought it up, so it was definitely *his* baby.

They had argued back and forth without resolving anything until Whit disappeared to get more supplies for lunch. By noon, he hadn't returned. Also by noon, Rocky had finished her third straight vodka.

Z. appeared again. "FOUR CHICKEN LIVERS. Cheep. Cheep," he mimicked: brandied chicken livers were the least expensive entrée on the lunch menu. "Got my order for table two—stuffed eggplant and a crab Louis?"

She hadn't.

"Well, how about the two soups?"

This she could manage. He whipped off with them. "Forks, we're running out of forks. Most restaurants have lots of forks."

I started washing up the silverware.

"TROUT WITH BACON STUFFING. STILL NEED A CRAB LOUIS AND A RATATOUILLE."

Rocky wrestled with the pots and pans, spilling things, swearing, muttering. Since Whit had been seen in the vicinity, Z. wasn't taking orders for sandwiches, so I had relatively little to do except keep up with the dishes and silverware there in the eye of the storm.

"FOUR CHICKEN LIVERS. SPIN-MUSH." Z. meant spinach-mushroom salad. "WHERE ARE MY ORDERS? It's getting ugly out here."

More crashing and banging. The sound of a bottle opening, glugging.

"TWO SOUPS. TWO RATATOUILLE. Where's Whit? I can't seat people and wait on them too."

"Shall I dish up the ratatouille?" I asked Rocky. *While you start on the livers,* I added silently.

"Leave them Rat Tits to me. I can do 'em." She couldn't find the slotted spoon, so she dished up with a ladle, sloshing watery trails over the prep table and plate. "Fucking Jesus. What did he order? You stay over there."

"He wants chicken livers. Four orders." I went through the tickets. "No, eight." I got the livers out of the refrigerator. When I opened the plastic container the smell hit me. "They're bad. Oh, God, they stink." Of all the bad spoiled smells, chicken livers are the worst.

Rocky stood with her head hanging forward, swaying.

"Bad," I repeated. "Not good."

"Nasty little fuckers." Her head lowered as if she planned to charge the plastic container. "Nasty, goddamn little fuckers."

Z. appeared. "Oh, my God." He stepped between Rocky

and the bad livers. "Rocky," he began in an artificially calm voice, "Rocky, dear, there are more chicken livers upstairs in the freezer. We'll get you some." He stroked her arm.

"Nasty goddamn fuckers." She reached for the bottle.

Z. intervened. "Now, Rocky, love, maybe you'd enjoy getting out of the kitchen for a few minutes? Just wait in the dining room for a little while, okay?"

She left the kitchen and headed for the bar. "QUICK," Z. said, shoving me to Rocky's side of the kitchen. "Dish up these goddamn orders."

He herded me toward the stove. "I'm not going out there again without food in my hands." He snatched the dishes as soon as I'd slopped a little food on them. I threw parsley at his retreating back, as if some might reach the ungarnished platters.

The hum in the dining room seemed louder, more threatening. Had the sight of food gotten up their blood lust? I shuffled through the orders, then shoved a trout into the microwave. How long to cook it? Rocky had never let me touch any of the entrées, had guarded their preparation like a sacred rite. Two minutes? Three? Four? Where was the stuffing? I looked at the menu. Bacon stuffing? Shit. I yanked the fish out of the microwave and threw the bacon in. With another hand, I reached across the kitchen, around the corner and into the shelf where the stuffing mix lay; with my extra two arms I finished garnishing a crab Louis, dished up four soups, found there were only three left, poured them all back into the pot, added a can of chicken broth, and dished them up again. With my toes, I whipped cream, sliced more tomatoes, washed forks and plates, and rang for Z. to come pick up his orders.

I have always performed well under pressure.

Z. arrived and left in waves of hysteria. "HAHAHA-HAHA. Two MORE chicken livers. People think they can get chicken livers just because they're on the menu. HA-HAHAHAHA."

Rocky sat heavily at the bar. Every time the bell rang, she raised her head and tried to remember something. I hoped it wouldn't come to her.

From the way Z. went off into hysterical bursts of laughter whenever someone mentioned chicken livers, the customers were beginning to get the idea that perhaps they should order something else. "Ready any minute now," he lied over and over.

We were coming closer. I had gotten a rock-hard bag of livers out of the freezer and between the orders for trout, managed to thaw them, although a few exploded, painting gray splotches all over the inside of the micro-wave. They spat and hissed at me angrily in the pan as I sautéed them.

"Nasty little fuckers," I murmured as I poured brandy over them and struck a match. WHOOOSSH. Flames shot upward, bringing Z. and the busboy racing into the kitchen. "I guess you don't generally use that much brandy." I stirred the livers dramatically, although the heat seared my hand. "Nothing like a flaming dish. Heh. Heh."

Then two more people crowded into the room. Whit and Jules. Their arms full of packages, eyes full of anger. They had been fighting, tearing at each other all the while Z. and I had been trying to get lunch out. Whit made little clucking noises while Jules started to put away his groceries.

I felt absolutely triumphant as I dished out the last orders: ten chicken livers, actually six since the first four people who had ordered them had long since gone away. Not that anyone had told me they'd gone before I cooked the livers, but at that point, who cared? Lunch was over.

But not the excitement.

The fight between Whit and Jules must have been worse than usual, for they both carried a charge high enough to set off the smoke alarm. Jules's face, usually so beautiful, appeared downright ugly: eyes narrowed and mean, mouth drawn and set. Whit didn't look any better. With a tumbler full of straight bourbon, he came back into the kitchen to find out what had happened.

"Busy lunch?" Whit asked.

Clearly neither of them wanted or needed a restaurant crisis at that moment, but it wriggled before them. Then it loomed: Rocky lurched into the kitchen. For a moment, all went quiet, even the dining room outside. Rocky looked at me standing on "her" side of the little room, cooking at "her" stove. A kind of growl started deep in her throat. "Took over my kitchen," she said to Whit. "That sneaky bitch got me drunk and took over my kitchen. Tried to, anyway." She heaved herself toward me. "Out," she said. "Get out of my kitchen."

Jules cowered in the pantry area, but the word *my* got to him. "It's not your kitchen," he said, evenly advancing. "It's not YOUR fucking kitchen."

If she'd been a little more sober she would have known not to push him. But she could barely stand, much less think. Pickled.

She towered over me, pushing me toward the hot stove. "I want her out of this kitchen." I tried to stay absolutely still. Fear gave me a small furry animal's awareness.

"Rocky!" Whit called her name sharply. As she turned toward him, I escaped sideways. Whew. Enough of being small and furry. "Rocky. It's time to go home now."

"S'not. Gotta get things straight first." Rocky swayed. "Had this li'l problem today at lunch. Nothing 'portant. Li'l disagreement with you 'bout brunch. You're right, tho. I'll work brunch. Yep, come in on Saturday. Work brunch."

As if that were the only thing involved.

She smiled hazily at everyone, her mood having shifted. All, in her mind, was back to normal. She could go home and sleep it off.

Fire her, I beamed willfully toward Jules. *Fire her now while there is a chance.* But I could feel Jules retreating, his anger dissipating, that cornered look coming on again. Still, he had actually stood up to her briefly, they'd all seen it. *Fire her,* I urged again. *It's your restaurant, YOUR restaurant.*

"This is MY restaurant," Jules began unevenly.

"OUR restaurant," Whit put in, angry again.

"It's a shithole." Rocky picked up the anger, magnified and returned it. Seeing Jules back down had gotten her bully up.

"Out." Jules, in a little voice, had actually said it. "Everybody just get out of here."

Rocky started toward the door, toward the porch. "Good idea," she said evenly. "I could use a drink." By her lights, she certainly hadn't been fired, just ordered out of the kitchen. She at least had enough sense to leave. But couldn't, for there were too many people in the small room. Her heavy jacket swept the plate of leftover chicken livers across the table and sent it all splattering down the front of Whit's new pants.

"Goddamn it, Rocky. You're falling-down drunk." Whit tried to wipe his ruined trousers. Rocky picked up a dirty towel and began to rub Whit's crotch. High, hysterical laughter came from Jules but was cut short as Whit drew back in rage: "Don't you touch me, cunt."

It was real now.

And very quiet. Rocky, suddenly uncertain, drew back. "You talk to me like that and I'll quit. I'll fucking quit."

"Go ahead," Whit dared her. She looked instinctively toward Jules to save her.

All hung fire.

Go ahead, I thought toward Jules. *Kill.*

"Good idea," Jules said.

"What did you say?!" She reared over him, menacing. But Jules stood his ground with gentle dignity.

"I said, 'Good idea,'" he repeated, even more firmly.

"Good idea!! And after all my mother did for your father."

"All she ever did for him was to screw him," Whit said nastily. "And we're tired of paying for it."

"What did you say?"

"I said, Ms. Rocky, that the party is over. It's a good idea for you to leave now."

"I'll show you what's a good fucking idea," Rocky shouted, picking up a bus pan of dirty dishes and throwing them onto the floor so hard the sound of breaking glass almost drowned out her roar. "This is a good idea.

And this." She tore the worn apron in half, then ripped the halves into strips, causing frightful linen screams.

"This is an even fucking better idea." She threw the grease can against the upended cartons where the spices were kept, sending them all crashing to the floor. Cooking oil flowed over spilled heaps of basil and oregano while rancid bacon grease lay in clots among broken glass. A ten-dollar bottle of saffron teetered on the edge and then plopped over into the mess below.

Whit, Jules, and I stood immobile and wide-eyed, partly in fear, partly in awe. Something primeval had been unleashed in the kitchen. Rocky's face was almost unrecognizable, her eyes flat, unseeing, the veins of her neck standing out, pulsing.

She picked up a tray of desserts from the serving port, carried it down the passage and, stopping at the doorway, heaved it into the dining room, splattering the frightened customers at nearby tables. Before anyone could react, she charged out into the dining room and began to pull the blue-gray cloths off every table within reach. "Good idea," she shouted to the astounded guests, bringing crockery, food, flowers, utensils, and wine down onto their laps or the floor. "Fucking good idea." She worked her way to the door leaving a wake of breakage, spillage, and fear behind her.

The door slammed with an incredible bang. About 5.4 on the Richter scale.

"Do you suppose," Jules's voice quavered slightly in the shocked silence, "that means she quit?"

FIFTEEN

Transcending Dualism While Whipping Egg Whites into High, Stiff Peaks

AFTER A YEAR at Dorje Ling, my funds were running low. Reading a newsletter from a college in the area, I saw a notice for a job in women's studies. Over an hour's drive away, but manageable, definitely manageable. Maybe it was time to think about going back to the university, at least part time. Time to apply some of the Dharma teachings in the outside world.

The kitchen, overrun recently by teenagers on retreat, was driving me crazy. Sometimes Dorje Ling seemed even smaller than the little southern town where I'd grown up. In fact, one of the lama's wives sometimes referred to Dorje Ling as "the plantation." That self-enclosed quality disappeared when we had large retreats and events, but grew worse when everyone there just sort of stewed together in isolation. The difference being that at Dorje Ling we all knew that the negativity was rooted in our own projections and (ideally) worked with this.

After I set up the interview, I didn't have any better sense than to actually look forward to it. Poor child aquiver with anticipation about coming home to women's studies, to feminism, to a female community. I'd been cooking too long; I wanted back into teaching. Back to something normal while I digested the tremendous download of Buddhist teachings that I'd received over the last few years. But again, it was already too late for normalcy. I just didn't know that yet.

When I tried to review recent research in women's studies, I was surprised at the airless, claustrophobic quality I picked up. I'd taught Women in Literature during my first year in California, but had switched to the writing program, so I had a lot to catch up on, though women's studies had been my specialization in graduate school in what now seemed like the Dark Ages. An article written by one of the women on the interview committee—a statistical analysis of women in the workforce in Baltimore in the thirties—was imaginatively entitled "A Statistical Analysis of Women in the Work Force in Baltimore, Maryland, between 1930 and 1939." Most of the writings were dominated by an abstract, meanly technical vocabulary. Everything seemed to be about language, nothing about women. What had happened to the body? The emotions? The real issues? And what on earth were they talking about? What had happened to feminism while I was cooking here in the trenches? The general tone of hostility should have been a warning. Instead, I thought of myself as a lamb returning to the fold.

And I found myself in a wolves' den: sitting on a metal chair in a conference room, ringed by three females with open folders on their laps.

"A chef?" The pack leader looked at me blankly. She reminded me of a milder, better-dressed version of Rocky, but with the same piggy eyes, combative stance, and oppressive heaviness.

"You cook?" The second in command frowned. "Food?"

The third woman seemed interested, even sympathetic, but remained silent. The three of them were dressed in severely cut business suits, in varying shades of gray or navy. All had the same closed air of self-inflicted superiority that I had hated in my male professors. I had to fight back tears. This isn't what I'd wanted for women's studies, this bitchy recapitulation of male academics. I—all of the women back then—had wanted it to be something new, vital, real. *Authentic* was a word we all had not just used, but experienced viscerally. And *community*. I remembered how my first women's studies class got together at my house and we'd cooked a huge Indian meal. I'd shown them how to roll out parathas ("Hey, sir, is this going to be on the exam?"), which we'd fried until golden, then eaten with a chutney made from fresh coconut mixed with lime juice and green peppers. One of the students had forgotten to put the cover over the mustard seeds, and when they started popping all over the stove, we shrieked and squealed, bumping into each other trying to find a top. Then collapsed in a heap, laughing. I bet these women didn't invite their students home for a meal. They probably couldn't even cook. The sense of loss was so acute that I had to turn the catch in my throat into a cough.

"Well, yes." I tried forced brightness through my misery. Maybe underneath the stony stares these women were still there somewhere. "Actually, I've found the kitchen quite useful in thinking about gender," I told the blank faces around me, hearing myself slip back into my above-it-all tone. "I did my dissertation about the ways in which . . ."

I remembered all the heartbreaking work I'd put into writing "Feminism and Dualism," a subject with neither end nor mercy. The first part of the dissertation outlined how a feminist argument springs up when opposed ideas of masculine and feminine become polarized, how feminist thought and action struggle to rebalance these forces, to overcome stasis. I had come to the unfortunate conclusion that feminists, although they started out seeking balance, had found power in their position and weren't able to move on. I had come to see the women's movement as a freeway exit, leading from a dualistic highway to an exchange with many paths and possibilities. But all too often women camped out on the exit, thinking that was the end, the destination. This only mired everyone deeper into dualism. I also suspected that academic prose itself was "masculine," so that anytime I opened my mouth to spout theory, whatever I'd really meant to say about the feminine side of things became hideously distorted and fragmented. (Later I learned that in Tibetan Buddhism, the feminine is ground and anything that comes up into form is masculine.) I had been careful not to mention any of this in my actual writing or in conferences with my adviser or other committee members.

Working with a largely gay staff at Lafayette's, I couldn't help realizing that most of my theorizing about gender had been full of shit. Or at least of vast ignorance. At the restaurant, gender was not only bent, but pretzelized into amazing combinations. My basic argument had been that if human beings were freed from polarized gender roles, they could become androgynous. This I loftily equated with being fully human. But, for all of my fine words written at the university, for all that they'd granted me a degree, at the time I hadn't known jack about gender.

While working at the restaurant, I'd think a lot about the dissertation that I didn't have time to write. One day when making a chocolate mousse, I'd carefully separated the yolks from the whites, putting them each in their own identical gray bowls, fat yellow moons and a little glaucous sea. Gently sprinkled sugar over the thick, rich yellows, adding dark chocolate melted with butter. As I stirred, the egg mixture darkened, thickened. I whipped the whites in the other bowl until they stood frothy and unspotted, the purest white. In contrast, the container of dense chocolate seemed laden with the dark sexuality of some brooding seducer in a fin de siècle drawing.

Visually, at least, the contents of the two bowls loomed up as opposites, as yin and yang, one light, dry, the other dark, heavy, wet. But which should be called the male, which the female? I'd seen the white purity as virginal female, but in Taoism, the woman would be aligned with the wet darkness of yin. If we go from West to East, do we switch the alignments of masculine and feminine? And what of the values attributed to each side? Would the passivity and masochism the Freudians assigned to women in the West be seen as Eastern virtues of equanimity and compassion? And then? What else would change? Everything?

As I moved on to the final step of combining the mousse, folding the heavy brown globs into the stark purity of the egg whites, the commingled mixture took on its own creamy texture in a willing seduction, became an orgy of pleasures as the dark entered the whites and the envaginated light penetrated and enfolded and merged with the dark.

Soon I'd forgotten about opposites altogether, disappearing into the action. Mixing, remembering how men and women merge as seamlessly as yin and yang become the Tao. Mixing, understanding why the union of man and woman goes beyond thought of self and other.

Mixing, mingling. Skin on skin, fur on fur, tongue on nipple. Goat leg sliding goat leg. Down, backward, falling though the trapdoors of self, into the river of male and female together . . . loving, mating, bonding without thought of hesitation, no more able to keep separate boundaries than the egg whites and the chocolate coming together in shared wetness and fecundity could ever again live apart.

I understood then that it didn't matter which side is called masculine, which feminine, but as long as I viewed them as opposites I would continue to create—and strive to overcome—dualism after dualism. Only when I disappeared into the action, when I myself became the mixing, enfolding dark into white, did I free myself from a sense of separation, opposition, alienation.

For a long while after that, every time I'd try to theorize about feminism and dualism, my thoughts would still harden and turn gray, like chocolate that has been left too long in the cold. But I understood it all that afternoon in the hot restaurant kitchen.

Then the dreams started. Every night I dreamed a pattern of two, three, five. Two lanterns would turn into three lanterns, then five and, almost immediately, multiple lights. Two flowers would become three, five, a field. It took me a while to realize the dream code beneath the images, but it kept repeating night after night until I finally noticed.

But what did it mean? I had the feeling that nightly my unconscious was waving to me—all but shouting *yoo-hoo*—with the way out of dualism. If the dream had stopped at three, I would have been fine: thesis, antithesis, synthesis. I'd quoted Hegel enough to have him show up nightly in my dreams, but what was with the five, then multiplicity? That the Hegelian dialectic extended to an endless loop the Western mind kept getting stuck in?

In one particularly vivid dream, the twos and threes were clouds. When I got to the multiplicity part that night, for the first time I noticed not the number of clouds, but the sky behind them.

When I went into the sky, I felt a sense not only of opening into vastness, but of being connected with everything contained within it. That's what my dreams had been trying to tell me. Not the figure, but the ground. Nondual at last. And this was before I started studying Buddhism, but one of a series of hints, messages that my unconscious kept sending me.

At the women's studies interview, I'd planned to go on about this research, or rather to *start* talking about it, but the second wolf—the one in navy—broke in. "You've published this work?"

"Not yet," I explained. "I've been writing other things. In fact, I'm working on a cookbook . . ."

"A cookbook?"

All three closed their folders in unison.

As I walked across the campus to my car, feeling strangely light, I remembered how many things I'd slipped out of, sidled away from. Marriages, relationships, jobs, plans, careers. Always leaving. And the things that I didn't abandon—like my academic career—left me. Just suddenly not there anymore. Not that I planned or plotted. But from one minute to the next, old things were over. New things began.

Death must be like that, I thought. Goodbye to one lifetime, one dream. Now you see me, now you don't. "That reality is no longer operative," as Richard Nixon used to say.

But, I thought as I drove around and around the campus looking for the exit, there is bound to be a gap between the dying of one reality and the arising of another, an opening, a crack to slip through. They'd talked about it at Dorje Ling. Into what? Silence? Peace? Heaven? The ground of being? Buddha nature? I pulled into the parking lot to look at the campus map which seemed to have no relation whatsoever to the territory I'd been circling.

The gap, that was the key, the gap that led to skylike emptiness. Like rising in bread, like pinholes in a soufflé. Like space between words. I cranked up my car and drove straight to the right exit, heading out.

SIXTEEN

Relaxing the Mind

NO ONE is in a hurry today. Lynn is working on the rolls for dinner, flattening circles of dough, cutting them into pie-shaped wedges, then rolling them up and twisting the ends toward each other like a croissant. Maya is our kitchen help. Lynn has been telling her about her days of cooking in a senior center. *Bland* was the operative word there, according to Lynn. They didn't even *buy* pepper. When I tell them about the erotic decorations that Jules used for his "special occasion" French chocolate cakes, Lynn gets the idea that she'll roll dough out into eternal knot designs and decorate a few buns. In the meantime, Maya and I are prepping vegetables for the salad bar, which we'll store in water in the cold room. An endless job, but in the days to come we'll be grateful to have so much of the work already done.

Diane, the head chef at Dorje Ling, complains that when she gets obsessed by small things (or big ones, when available), her world narrows. To her lack of closet space, to what her son said to her on the phone, to the way the pantry is organized. Always something. She says her mother is the same way, also her daughter. With her mom it is little things that people have said to her. She teases out hidden messages, slights, insults. With the daughter, it's clothes. She doesn't have a navy slip to match her new navy skirt, she saw one on sale at Ross, maybe if she went there during her lunch break she could buy it. And look for a navy belt that is only an inch wide. The one she has is almost two inches, et cetera. Endless details of dress or home decoration dominate her life. Whatever we attend to becomes our reality.

Recently Diane went down to the garden to get away from the kitchen and the problem we were having with the delivery from a natural foods place in Oregon, which she'd been fixating on all week. When she got back, she still looked tense and wound up.

"How's the garden?" Lynn asked. "What's in bloom down there? Are the tomatoes coming in? Have the deer broken through the fence again?" People in the kitchen are always hungry for news from outside.

Diane came to a dead halt with this funny look on her face. "I didn't see a thing. Not one single thing in the garden." No need to tell us that her thoughts had circled round and round the delivery problem, the supplier, the lists, the details.

"Go again."

"Too much to do."

"Go."

This time she came back relaxed, easy. "Suckers all over those tomatoes, but the fence seems to be holding the deer back. I sprayed the edges." Deer don't like artificial smells, so we'd been spraying the top of the fence with cheap deodorant we kept in the garden shed. She'd picked a bouquet of wild delphiniums, which she put in a glass near the phone. As she worked through the problems with the supplier, she twirled one of the flowers in her hand, tracing the outline of the petals with her fingertips, holding it up to the light, filling her eyes with its blueness.

Jules and I sometimes used to get into a similar dreamy, relaxed mode when we cooked together in the afternoons. Prepping for dinner as his helper became my favorite part of the day. Jules, for all his deceits and moods—which, I soon found, were legendary—was a true genius in the kitchen. He rarely instructed me on how to do anything, but I learned more from watching him work with food than from reading dozens of cookbooks. Now, in the kitchen of the buddhas, I see that Jules could access an in-the-moment state called *rol-pa* in Tibetan. When you're writing on water, you can see the letters coming into being and going out of being simultaneously. To move with the point of the stick is *rol-pa*. Or visualize silk flowing smoothly over the edge of a tabletop. To stay with the sense of turning is *rol-pa*.

I heard one teacher say *rol-pa* is something that you can be but not have. The moment you say to yourself, "Now I've got it," it's gone, snapped back into a dualistic mode of self and object through remembering "I."

What he said about *rol-pa* is similar to descriptions of what we in the West call the timeless present, the flow, the ongoing moment of now. To learn our place in this ever changing stream and stay in that groove is to remain in a state of calm abiding. Some people learn this on a meditation cushion. I learned it in the kitchen, so many kitchens, most pleasurably from cooking with Jules in the afternoons.

The constant stream of intense taste sensations grounded me then, providing a physical rather than mental reference for being. When I was working with food—slicing green peppers, mincing onions, paring zucchini—life became real. The color, smell, feel, taste of food provided a link to the physical world that I focused on with total concentration as great frozen chunks of my inner world broke apart and fell away.

Never before had I experienced the luxury of letting myself completely empty out. Or had the privacy in which to do so. Nobody in the restaurant seemed interested in me or my situation. Within the first month at Lafayette's, I found that my own story didn't hold anyone's attention for over fifteen or twenty seconds. Nobody cared to hear about a promising university career cut off at the knees, ex-husbands, ex-lovers, any of the rest of it. At Lafayette's I'd reached a state of bland anonymity that I found extremely peaceful.

Later on I found that one of the things that keep us fixated in our ordinary mind is a tendency to reify the self. The antidote, or one of them, is to lie still as a corpse in a charnel ground for a month. Confused mind being the biggest and closest charnel ground of them all.

One of the main things I liked about working in the restaurant was that sense of being nobody. Credit from my academic achievements didn't transfer into the kitchen; my sexuality (sun and moon in Scorpio) came up negative in this largely gay community. Most of my friends had been left behind or to my penultimate husband. So there I was in that kitchen, happening, but outside of a context that I understood or that understood me in the "normal" ways. Because of the speed and the action, because of the nonreification of an identity, working in the kitchen evoked a different sense of time, that of being intensely present in the moment. Here. Now. Look this way.

SEVENTEEN

Bread

THERE'S SOMETHING quite wonderful about making bread. You can't bully it, for one thing; you just have to cooperate with the process. Turn, press, fold. Add a little more flour. Turn, press, fold. I don't think bread worries about its own performance, doesn't ask the cook, "Am I doing this the right way? Does the rye bread know more than I do?" It just gives itself over to whatever process has taken it in hand. Trusts it to continue.

Standing at the counter, I thought, as I often did, about Julie, gone now for six months. Lynn said she dreamed about the child almost every night. Sometimes Julie was still alive and they were just driving around in the truck, going to the library or getting groceries. Normal things. Other times Lynn knew that Julie was dead. She'd come back and hold Lynn, comfort her. Or Lynn would hold her. "It's hard to say who is who in the dream," Lynn told me. "But I'm always so grateful when she shows up."

I had dreamed about Julie only once, but it had that special shimmering quality of an important dream. I had been standing at the kitchen counter in my dream when I felt the little girl suddenly standing beside me, rubbing her face into my leg. Julie had been smiling, flooded with light. A different Julie, but recognizable.

"Julie!" I'd said, "Where did you come from?"

Julie had put her finger against her lips. "Shhh," she'd whispered to me. "Shhhh." Hugged me, did her old double-hop out the door, and was gone.

Just that, nothing else.

I couldn't figure it out, but I'd gone silent. Hadn't spoken a word since then. I kept waiting for other dreams, signs. Nothing. Nada. Nor did I ask any of the lamas about it.

Quiet as rising bread. Trusting my own process to let me know when to speak again. It would signal an important transition, I could feel that. But what?

Lama P. finally noticed how silent I had been lately, brought his fingers to his mouth in a little locking motion, then looked at me questioningly. I nodded, he nodded, and that was that.

Few people talk to me now. I feel that I'm becoming transparent, more insubstantial by the day.

Silence, a stilling of not only the voices outside but the inner voices, the roof brain chatter. Now, without the babble of words—inner and outer—I watch my mind, notice when a thought arises. I turn my attention inward, asking, "Who is thinking this thought?" As the mind turns to look, the thinker seems to disappear. But a focus comes from the asking, a clearing, a deepening. No "me," but a presence. Awareness.

Even during my career as professional chef, I would listen closely to the undersound of the kitchen, searching for the presence of a larger order. When people insisted on talking, I couldn't hear the food. But *hear* is the wrong word, for food isn't audible or even audile, yet it does communicate. If you let yourself quietly *be* with food, something else takes place, something just outside the usual range of the senses, another order, another way of being. The *it* takes over. The me is gone.

When I first worked in a restaurant, I used to daydream of a mute helper, someone who had no interest whatsoever in speaking. She (I could somehow never imagine a man in this role) wouldn't tell about her plans for her vacation, the fights with her mother, the ins and outs of her most recent relationship. In my daydream of a mute helper, I was envisioning a future version of myself, of course. My imagination was sending directions, subtle hints as to how to proceed. How to glimpse sky, how to open into vastness. The odd thing is that in addition to this sense of spaciousness, I'm starting to feel close to people, to understand and sympathize with them on a new level, to participate in their lives in unexpected ways, to notice those around me as something more than irritants, as subjects rather than objects.

I had once heard Lama Tashi say that we have three minds, positive, negative, and natural mind. Sometimes a gap occurs in the Ping-Pong game of positive and negative and we glimpse natural mind. I was finding that sustained silence led me to experience natural mind directly. While talking about it drove the state farther and farther away.

Why is it I have to learn the same things over and over? When will it all come together, I wondered, putting the bread in the oven. Won't I ever be done?

EIGHTEEN

Naming

"DO YOU KNOW what happened to my friend Sarah in San Francisco? She's one of these very modern people who wants to stay completely in control of everything. One time Rinpoche was down there giving a public lecture and since I'd talked about him for years, she condescended to go hear him. As she sat in the auditorium, she opened her mind to him, mentally saying, 'Okay, I've heard a lot about you. Show me what you've got.' Immediately, like a bolt of lightning that almost threw her back in her chair, the response came into her thoughts: 'I don't have to show you a thing.'"

"Guess he showed her."

"That's what she said. Scared her to death. Ran away as fast as she could."

That night, I reread my favorite Rumi poem.

Chickpea to Cook

A chickpea leaps almost over the rim of the pot
where it's being boiled.

"Why are you doing this to me?"

The cook knocks him down with the ladle.

"Don't you try to jump out.
You think I'm torturing you.
I'm giving you flavor,
so you can mix with spices and rice
and be the lovely vitality of a human being.

Remember when you drank rain in the garden.
That was for this."

Grace first. Sexual pleasure,
then a boiling new life begins,
and the Friend has something good to eat.

Eventually the chickpea
will say to the cook,
            "Boil me some more.
Hit me with the skimming spoon.
I can't do this by myself.

I'm like an elephant that dreams of gardens
back in Hindustan and doesn't pay attention
to his driver. You're my cook, my driver,
my way into existence. I love your cooking."

The cook says,
            "I was once like you,
fresh from the ground. Then I boiled in time,
and boiled in the body, two fierce boilings.

My animal soul grew powerful.
I controlled it with practices,
and boiled some more, and boiled
once beyond that,
                    and became your teacher."*

During the next few days, I read this poem to so many people that everyone started calling me Chickpea.

"That's it, that's your Dharma name," Diane announced one day.

Most of the people who came to Dorje Ling adopted or were given a Buddhist name. Some even shaved their heads when this happened, but I thought that was carrying things a bit far.

"No, no it's not." Ever since my friend Linda had been dubbed Palden Lhamo after one of the Tibetan protectors, I'd wanted to be given a Dharma name as well. I'd been secretly hoping for Tara like the female Buddha, or Khandro, which means sky-dancer. But Chickpea?

Lama P.—to whom I'd read the poem twice—paused on his way through the kitchen. "It's perfect."

"Why?"

"Suits you," he said, raising his cup in a little toast. "Chef Chickpea."

Diane and Lynn raised their cups as well, beaming. So much for being named after a deity or a *bodhisattva*. As my hopes for being high and holy dissolved once again, I recognized Chef Chickpea as my true name.

*Coleman Barks, trans., *The Essential Rumi* (San Francisco: HarperSanFrancisco, 1995). Reprinted with permission.

NINETEEN

A Cup of Tea

THE CHENS from Hong Kong are my morning helpers in the kitchen. Both have pale teal T-shirts, black cotton pants, golden skin. I watch them load the dishwasher, gliding to and from the prep table with quicksilver movements. Working together, their bodies move in a constant dance of communication, not touching, not plastered together the way couples in love tend to be, but lighter, finer, more subtle. The teachings are about to begin, so they disappear into the shrine room, skimming the floor.

My third new helper stays on in the kitchen to prepare lunch. Today's talk about relationships and the spiritual path comes crackling over the speakers in the kitchen, sounding as if from a distant planet.

This new helper is Leo Stein, a poet from New York. Big, bearlike, lots of face. His headful of wild curly black hair gives him a woolly look, as if he'd just come in off the steppes. His dark thick eyebrows and bushy salt-and-pepper beard complete the effect. Liquid brown eyes wild and gleaming, soulful and sad, intelligent and dumb. I like the way Leo manages to look lost and found at the same time.

I'm a little in love with Leo, in fact, but only from afar. For the first time in my life I don't go hurtling after someone but enjoy him from a silent distance. It will be all right with me if Leo is around only for another week, that we share this space together and he returns to his wife or girlfriend or whoever waits for him back east. Leo, I know, is not the sort of person to be without a woman for very long, no question about that. Not that he chases women at Dorje Ling, but he tends to bend toward any female standing nearby the way a cold man leans toward a fire.

"Relationship," says Lama S. over the speakers, "can be a spiritual path, just as celibacy is a path." I notice Leo has stopped washing dishes at this point so as not to miss a word. "Not everyone chooses to be celibate," the lama continues. Some of the lineages of Tibet are householders, people who pursue spiritual goals within the context of marriage and a family. Her own teacher had told her that she could spend years in solitary retreat or she could do it the quick way by practicing while living with her husband and child. "My teacher never gave me the option of going away and becoming holy," she says. "Life itself had to become my retreat.

"Most of the relationships in our country are based on a sort of ledger model," says Lama S. "I make you a cup of tea, but, on some level, somewhere, I'm expecting you to make me one in exchange. If a week or so goes by and I haven't gotten my cup of tea, then I start this angry little dialogue within myself about how 'you' aren't fulfilling 'my' needs. But any relationship that is founded on the idea that another person will make you happy is doomed from the very start. The only ones that will ever succeed are those that begin with the question 'What can I do to make the other person happy?'

"And this motivation needs to be the ground of the relationship, not just a temporary attitude that you adopt to make yourself seem like a good person. You really can't be waiting for that cup of tea to come back to you but must learn to give freely. A cup of tea, a smile, a little kindness, there is always something that we can offer. Only through our unimpeded generosity do we become happy.

"When you go into a room," she continues, "look around and see what you can do to help. If you make that your stance toward life, then you'll never need anything else. You'll not be thinking about *your* needs, *your* wants, *your* desires. The center of the universe has shifted a little from *you* to the outside. This can be done within a relationship, within the family, with the world at large. Give. Love. Help. But without wanting something back to balance the ledger. You'll find that this makes you deeply happy all the time."

When the teaching ended, I prepared Leo a cup of tea by the stove. The talk had made me want to be good. Not goody-goody or pretend-nice in any way. Just helpful.

When I turned to give the tea to Leo, I found him holding out a cup toward me at the very same instant. We looked at each other, then burst out laughing, swept together into a free and clear sharing of joy.

Leo will stop washing dishes or prepping vegetables to go and write something down. He covers paper towels, backs of labels, bits of masking tape with words. His writing is curly and unruly, just like his hair. I find a written-over napkin in the pantry with this scrap of a poem:

> To gaze into an empty room
> is not becoming Buddha.
> To feed a starving lion, Buddha
> gave up one of his precious lives.
> As a rabbit, as food,
> he leapt in the fire.
> We're paired to help,
> like hands, like feet.
> To gaze into an empty room
> is not becoming Buddha.

I read the poem over several times, fold it up and put it in my apron pocket. The next time I see Leo, I return it, making a little bow. He bows back, gesturing for me to keep the napkin. Just as when we gave each other the cups of tea, I have a sense that we are truly present with each other in some sort of unexplored dimension that has neither center nor circumference.

The next time I come into the kitchen, Leo has left another poem for me:

What Breathes Us

> Regards to the day, the great long day
> that can't be hoarded, good or ill.
> What breathes us likely means us well.
>
> We rise up from an earthly root
> to seek the blossom of the heart.

What breathes us likely means us well.

We are a voice impelled to tell
where the joining of sound and silence is.

We are the tides, and their witnesses.

What breathes us likely means us well.

That afternoon, the group at Dorje Ling received a teaching on attachment. According to the Buddhists, there are three root things that poison the mind: attachment, aversion, and ignorance. We see something, we want it, we attach ourselves to it. Or we see it, don't want it, push it away. In addition, we make judgments about it. It's good, it's bad.

And ignorance? It's the basis of both of the above. Ignorance is indulging in attachment and aversion, in not knowing any better, in thinking the duality we create in our own minds is real, solid, firm. Which it isn't. What we think of as our self isn't real either. Not that it isn't there. Something's there, but it's changing, coming into being, going out of being, each instant.

And what does this mean in terms of relationship? Well, several things, obviously. First of all, we tend to see the other person in terms of our attachment (I love you, stay with me always), as the *object* of our affections rather than a subject in his or her own right. We can be attached to objects but can love only subjects.

Furthermore, the self—myself, yourself, himself—is like the weather. Not real or solid, but happening. Sometimes the rain and hail dominate everything. Other times, the clouds are light and fluffy, lots of sky showing through. But it's always impermanent, always changing, never the same from minute to minute. In terms of relationships, if we pin our happiness to one particular weather system, we're in trouble. And vice versa. As objects, we're not allowed to change, to be changeable. We won't allow the other as an object to do so either.

What a miserable situation, Lama S. says. Of course so many relationships fail. Their destruction is built right into the ground rules. But if you change the way you think about the other person, then there is a chance not only to give happiness, but to experience it as well. Mind changes: everything changes.

It feels good to be in love again even though I know that Leo is only a catalyst for some larger process that has been working within me. I know now that being in love is not the point.

Leo is leaving today. He's been hanging around the kitchen wanting to talk to me, maybe to hug me goodbye. Perhaps to invite me to run away with him forever. I'll never know because I'm standing here at the counter and not going to look up until the very last minute. It is not for Leo that I'll break my vow of silence. I learned that in a dream last night.

In my dream Leo and I soak in a hot tub on a deck in the Berkeley Hills. It feels like we have been together for a long, long time. One of us barely has to finish a sentence for the other to know what is meant, felt.

His arm moves in slow motion toward the bowl of dark-skinned, ripe fruit set on Dutch blue tiles. Toward the house, the blue tiles are interspersed with white ones, an occasional red hexagonal thrown in. Near the edge of the deck, where it falls down what seemed hundreds of feet, a gigantic jade plant sits on a deep red tile plant shelf.

We soak. Nothing needed.

"It's like this," Leo leans back in the dream tub. "There are all these women. I'm in love with all of them. With you, too. Mainly with you right now. But there have been all these wives, girlfriends, daughters, sisters. My poems are all about women, did you know? My head is crowded with these female people. I dream about them. I surf the Internet and get involved with cyber-women, virtual girls. I wish I had a lifetime to spend with each, but I don't."

"Maybe you have parallel lives with all of them, all of us. In dreams. On different planets, whatever."

"Anything seems possible in a hot tub."

"Or in a dream."

He lets out a huge sigh and gets up on the blue tile steps. "Want another pear?"

He passes me the bowl of fruit.

"Thing is, Leo," I set the bowl aside, "I've been around the block once or twice myself. Lots of men in my life, so I understand what you're talking about. I truly do. I'm gone on you, too. But I don't think being 'in' love is the point. Loving, maybe. Union."

"Union, as in . . . ?"

But I don't answer him.

Leo has been night-dreaming about me, too. I can tell. For several days he's stood only inches from me as I work at the stove. These teachings on relationships wrap around us but also keep us apart. At least they stop me (and, I suspect, him) from jumping into a remake of the same old romantic movie.

I've heard people from the office talk about the letters and phone calls and e-mails that Leo receives every day.

All from someone named Laura. Each morning, Lynn delivers blue envelopes to him that smell like the perfume they stick in fashion magazines. He goes outside to read them, then walks round and round the statue as if he's running from someone or something.

That's a situation I'm not about to jump into. Not this time. There is more at stake here than a passing fancy.

But we keep having these moments, clear and free little moments, spaces where we meet, touch, separate. This may be all we will ever have, but at least we're really present, not lost in some drama of self, some fantasy of the other. We show up right there together in the kitchen.

And there he is. Leo, next to me. His arms around me, hugging me goodbye. He wants me to say goodbye to him, to say his name. I look him in the eye instead, then wiggle my fingers in a final wave.

What is important is loving, without the "in" part. Love. In a vast sort of way. Not that nose-to-nose, toes-to-toes business, but an ever expanding connection to the universe and all that it contains.

When Leo returns home, he sends such a beautiful love poem that I cry all the way through *puja*. Somehow I don't think I've seen the last of Leo Stein.

Within Another Life

Those whose days were grudging or confused
may come back trapped within another life

as a boulder, or a pane of glass,
or a door that suffers every time it's slammed.

If I return a boulder, love, some summer day
come sit by me and contemplate these horses and
these hills.

And if a windowpane, gaze through to see
the meadow on our walks where brown geese strut.

And if I am a door, come home through me,
be sure I'll keep you safe.

And if a knotted, twisted rope,
from long self-clenching and complexity,

oh love, unbind, unbraid me then
until I flow again like windswept hair.

TWENTY

Dzogchenpa among the Presbyterians

"I'LL COME AT ONCE," I said into the phone, practically the first words I'd spoken in months. Diane had handed me a message as soon as I'd walked into the kitchen after the long retreat. My mother had had a fall; she'd broken her hip. They needed me in South Carolina.

I'd been on a six-week *dzogchen* retreat in Oregon with Lama P. where we'd studied the nature of mind for three weeks, then meditated for three. We used a simple, formless meditation with no center, no circumference, just a steady awareness that is uncontrived and natural. To find this state and rest in it had been the goals of the retreat. I hated for the retreat to end, but when it's over, it's over.

"She's being perfectly ridiculous" was the first thing my sister-in-law Bitsy said to me. "Wants to go home. Says she doesn't need physical therapy when she can't even walk. Says she'll remember how once she gets back home. And I'm so busy with the wedding I can barely see." Bitsy had been planning her daughter's wedding since the poor child was born. "As much as I'd like to keep on doing *everything* for Rena Grace, I just can't. Not all the time."

"As I said, I'll be there as soon as I can get a flight. Is Mother in pain?"

"You haven't shaved your head, have you?"

"No, Bitsy, I haven't."

"Well, that's a relief. We were afraid that maybe you had. You're enough of an embarrassment as it is, being a heathen and all. And don't go putting up any statues in the house, either."

"Statues?" I was always amazed at what the family thought I might do. "You mean of Buddha?"

"Any idol. We're a Christian family. Rena Grace prays every night that I'll quit smoking and you'll get over being a Buddhist."

Oh, it's hard to remain in a natural, uncontrived state of mind when you hear things like this. Fortunately, the habit of silence came to my rescue as it would time and time again in the coming months.

There was no transition from deep, enriching silence to family crisis, to family concepts about me, about who they thought I was. It wouldn't matter what I said, what I did; they'd made up their minds about me long ago, worked it out over Sunday dinners and holiday meals when I'd been absent. Or so it felt. Coming from a retreat just then, I was acutely aware that my ordinary mind, *sem* in Tibetan, had a habit toward error, toward projection, toward imaginative interpretations of what other people were thinking and why. It's helpful when I write fiction but otherwise counterproductive. During retreat, I'd spent a fair amount of time just watching *sem* strut her stuff, but witnessing it in the context of a retreat can lead to change, transformation, purification.

When I called my brother to give him my flight information, he filled me in on the fall, the pin they had put into her hip, and her prognosis, which was surprisingly good. She'd fallen as she went to turn off the television in the den, hit her head on the brick fireplace, then dragged herself across the dining room and living room to the phone in her bedroom.

"If she'd been wearing her LifeLine, she could have just pressed the button." After our father died, my brother had arranged for this beeper that rang an emergency number. She was supposed to wear it on a neck cord, but Mother kept it neatly tucked into her bedside table drawer. "I pay for it every month. I don't see why she didn't have it with her. Not going to do a bit of good where it is. Isn't going to hurt herself if she falls in bed, for Christ's sake."

"She says it messes up her hair when she puts it on. And it makes her feel old to wear it."

"Well, damn it, she is old. Anyway, it was after two when she called me. I got there about the time the ambulance did, then she couldn't decide what to take with her to the hospital. You know how she is about her clothes. I kept bringing out all these outfits for her to choose from. Bitsy was down in Atlanta visiting Walker Junior that night, so it was all up to me. Awful. Finally, the ambulance driver said he thought she should take the pink suit and just kind of picked her up and took her out, even though she'd changed her mind by the time she got to the front door and wanted the blue one."

"Why come now? Mother will be in the hospital for another few weeks doing physical therapy, right?"

"Well, it's the dog, partly." Hatred of Baby Pinkums, probably the most ill-tempered Pomeranian ever to bare his teeth, was one of the few things I had in common with the rest of the family. "They won't let her bring Stinkums to the hospital or to Heather Gardens, that's where she's going for her month of physical therapy. She doesn't want the dog to go to a kennel."

So I wasn't being recalled to help take care of my mother, but to dog-sit? It just got worse and worse. If I were writing a novel, I wouldn't even put this in.

"And she doesn't like the food at the hospital."

She wanted me to bring her food, it turned out, lunch and dinner. Her cook of forty years had died two years before, leaving her bereft. "How could she," Mother had asked, her eyes thrown upward, "after all this time?" Since then Mother had eaten out whenever possible and resorted to Instant Breakfast and Cup of Soup when she had to "cook" at home.

"Bitsy moved some stuff out of the house." My brother sounded uncomfortable. "So it wouldn't get in your way."

"Stuff? What kind of stuff?"

"Just some of the blue and gold china. Some silver things."

"The Limoges set? Walker, that's on the top shelf in the butler's pantry. How could that be in my way? Does she think I'm going to steal the china? The silver?"

"Aw, now. You know how Bitsy is. She doesn't mean any harm."

I knew exactly how she was and, for my brother's sake, held my tongue.

When I tried to explain the family dynamics to Lama P. it came out all backward. How do you explain to someone raised in Oregon about a sister-in-law who wears decorated clothes? Her gardening outfits have gingham flower carts embroidered on them, with hats to match. At Christmas, she wears vests with snow scenes or Santas, and tiny bow-wrapped presents or tree ornaments as earrings. She even has four sets of Twelve Days of Christmas place mats that she changes daily for all twelve days. "Aren't they *precious*?" she cooed when she showed them to me. It is her most favorite word in the world. *Uncontrived* is not in her vocabulary.

"They'll show you your limits," Lama P. had said. "Test you. But that's okay. They need your help. You should go."

"Well, of course I'll go. But, um, the family is so . . ."

"Yes?"

"It's just that it takes me about twenty minutes to start hallucinating when I get there. I forget everything I've learned since I was twelve."

"Try to watch your mind. Watch to see where it gets caught, where it fixates."

"And I don't feel any compassion when I'm around them. Not the tip of a hair's worth."

"You don't have to *feel* compassion. You just have to *be* compassionate."

Two weeks later I sat in Mother's room at Heather Gardens, watching a rerun of *Murder, She Wrote*. She wouldn't watch it by herself, would drop the remote and ring for the nurse if I left the room for any reason.

"She left me here alone again," she'd tell the nurse when she finally answered the call, "with the bad TV."

We'd made the move from the hospital to the "assisted living facility" of Heather Gardens during the past week, bringing her Audubon prints from the house, her desk and bookcase, her favorite excruciatingly uncomfortable blue chair and footstool. Daily I brought clothes from her closet to the Gardens, but never the right ones.

"I think she's getting better," Bitsy whispered as we watched Mother nap one afternoon. Back to her old demanding, critical, impossible-to-please self was what we both meant. But that was a relief. The sight of the shrunken old lady in the hospital bed had shocked me. Being compassionate wasn't even an issue, I would have done anything in my power to have helped her. But what had become of the great adversary of my life? My worthy opponent in years and years of struggle for independence? Those years of defensive maneuvers and manipulations dropped away, leaving us both there in the fragile present.

"Of course I'm better," she said now, not even opening her eyes. "Not a thing in the world wrong with me except the bad TV. I do wish you and Walker had been kind enough to get the good TV."

After Walker told her about the different cable options, Mother had gotten it into her head that everyone else had "good TV," which they paid more for, but she'd gotten stuck with the bad kind.

"It's daytime TV," I tried to explain after Bitsy left.

"You've never watched television in the daytime before. It's all bad."

"No, I was in Mrs. Ellison's room and she had on the most interesting program. Came in here and couldn't get a thing. Bitsy talked Walker into getting the bad kind, I just know it."

"The program was probably over when you got back to your room."

"No, I came straight here." But it took her nearly half an hour to get from one room to another, since she had never mastered the wheelchair. She would drive herself into a corner and stay there until someone found her and wheeled her back to her room.

"I don't see why one of the maids can't just push me," she'd complain.

"Don't call them maids, Mother. It makes them mad. They are nurses."

"Oh, I doubt that. I doubt that very much. Fat as they are?"

Oh, she's getting better, my mother with the outrageous mouth and the uncompromising stance toward everything and everyone around her. But I'd caught a glimpse of the beast at the window that couldn't be unseen. Her sharp mind was going, was partly gone. Her body, well, it was just a matter of time. And not that much time, either.

I didn't use the formal Buddhist techniques: didn't visualize Tara above her head or mine; didn't do *tonglen*, breathing in her pain and sending her loving-kindness; didn't pray to the lama. But I did show up. I was with her when we sat in the garden in the afternoons, watching the birds. I was with her ailing, leaking body when she needed help and was ashamed to ask for it. I wasn't off in the past lost in concepts about her wrongs and my wrongs when she held out her hand to me. I was there, with her, when I took her hand.

TWENTY-ONE

On Having a Teacher

"WELL, HAVING A TEACHER isn't a matter of sitting down for a cup of tea and a cozy chat, you know."

A group of students just back from Nepal for *Drubchen* sat talking at the table outside the kitchen window. I could hear every word as I stood cleaning out the spice rack, grateful to be back at Dorje Ling after yet another trip to see my family. The whole time I'd been gone, something vital had been absent from my life, almost as if a color had gone missing from the spectrum.

"Hardly," put in a woman's voice. "Everything I thought about myself and my world got turned upside down on this trip. And it wasn't pretty. Sometimes I was hanging on for dear life."

"It's funny how it works, isn't it? I hardly talked to Rinpoche at all, but a sort of mirroring started taking place in my dreams, in meditation, in thoughts. I began to know things in a different way."

"What I don't understand," a new voice breaks in, "is why I cry so much when I go in to see him. All these loud, ugly sobs. And I'm not even unhappy."

"You, too?" Several voices here.

"Something to do with the emotional body breaking through." Lama P.'s voice.

I lean forward because I want to hear the rest of what he says, but a newbie comes up just then and joins the group.

"I don't think I'd ever let a teacher tell me what to do," the newbie proclaims. "Personal freedom is something I plan to hang on to." Her toss-my-curls-and-stamp-my-little-foot ego seems embarrassingly familiar to me.

"What happens with a teacher is not that he or she tells you what to do, but reveals who you are. Sometimes that is much harder to rebel against."

A pause.

"Of course, everyone's experience is very different," Lama P. says smoothly. "Some teachers are wrathful, others gentle. Some renowned wrathful teachers can be mild as milk with one student and not another. And the relationship itself goes through lots of different phases."

"Some teachers can be ego-driven and dangerous," Lonny warns. "Be careful. Watch them for a long time before you decide. See how they are with other people, about sex and about money. And what their other students are like."

"They will be watching you, as well. It's a two-way street."

"They will?" The newbie again.

"These lamas have powers we can't even begin to appreciate."

"We really need to have the blessings of the guru to make any spiritual progress." I don't recognize this soft female voice.

When one of the Rinpoches had come from Nepal last month, someone had asked him about the "blessings of the guru." The old Tibetan had answered that the guru gave you authentic teachings, you tested them out, and they worked. Those were the blessings of the guru.

Sometimes it's hard to be a Westerner with our habit toward doubt and suspicion. The people I'd seen at the center whose only practice was devotion often seemed the happiest. Certainly easy to be around, generally helpful.

When I first came to Dorje Ling, questions would bubble up but there would be no one to talk to about them. Everyone there was inside the box, so to speak. Everything in the system was explained by something else inside the system. On bad days I'd think that I'd fallen into some sort of supercult for overachievers. On good days, I'd feel that I was blessed to have heard any of the teachings and that it was my own fault if I couldn't incorporate them into my life or mind. Most days were somewhere in between.

In time I decided that it's all right that I couldn't accept everything exactly as it was imported from Tibet. Our transitional generation of Buddhists is supposed to ask questions, probe, examine. That's our karma. But wouldn't it be better to do it step-by-step rather than suddenly swallowing the whole thing at once, then choking and/or spitting it out?

Be patient, Lama P. tells us. With yourself, with the teachings. Test them out, see if they bring you benefit. When they do, you get a little more faith, then you can go deeper. Prayer helps.

Few of the senior students will talk about their strug-
gles, but Lonny told me that more than once she's
stripped her walls bare, taken down all the pictures of the
deities and the teachers. Then she'll start over at the beginning, vowing not to create harm. She'll sit on her
cushion in silence for a half-hour every day. Just sitting,
following her breath. At a certain point, when it feels authentic, she'll add the vow to help others.

Now in her fifties, Lonny has been a Buddhist student
since a trip to Nepal in the seventies. She met a teacher,
now one of the regular ones at Dorje Ling, and has
worked with him closely since then. Sometimes, she later
told me, it was just too much, too Tibetan, too foreign,
too just plain weird. But then after she'd dismantled her
shrine, she'd let her mind settle into that state of pristine
awareness her teacher had first pointed out to her, rest in
what he'd called natural mind. Deeper than any state of
mind she'd ever experienced in her whole life, more
meaningful than any of the pleasures she'd been taught
to pursue. She'd touch this ground of being and feel a
swell of gratitude for the people, the long lineage that
had nurtured and preserved the methods for going there.
Then she'd put back up a picture of her teacher. Then her
teacher's teacher. She'd start doing a little practice,
prayers to Tara maybe, then her statues would be turned
back around and the cycle would start over again.

By now at least I know enough not to reject the whole
and start picking out only the parts I like. I too have
come to respect lineage, to see wisdom in a living tradition. The New Age fluff balls I've encountered recently

make me doubly appreciative of an established method, one designed to curb, not cushion, the ego. I see the positive effects all around me in the senior students who are able to embody the teachings. How could I not have faith in the system that trained them?

Yesterday I heard from a colleague in the university's writing program. She and the newest chairman, a mutual friend, had been talking about an upcoming opening for the spring quarter. Very short notice, but it would be nice, the note said, to have someone they already knew and liked. Why didn't I apply? Where was I, anyway?

The coded message here was that there had been yet another coup in the writing program and my colleagues were looking for people who would support them. I could still weasel my way back into teaching if I wanted to.

Did I care?

Decisions are made through the way the questions are asked, of course, so I rephrased different versions of my situation to myself.

How could I go back to teaching when I no longer believed in words? When I've learned the rich wisdom of silence at last? Even not teaching, why should I go back to Samsara-by-the-Sea and arrange the day around meeting a friend for wine and cheese, then going on to the newest restaurant for dinner? Maybe tucking in a Buddhist lecture somewhere if it wouldn't strain the schedule? No, I hadn't forgotten how quickly an endless round of pleasure palled, or how empty it left me to simply seek sensation after sensation. Did I want to die and say I was really good at pursuing pleasure? Death might come tomorrow. Didn't I want to find out what this life is all about, before it was over?

I don't aspire to enlightenment, but I hope to get just a little bit farther beyond this dream of self. What are human beings for? What's the point of having a human mind and body except to learn, to help, to love?

Cooking is a process that is irreversible. It's too late for me to go back to being raw, too late to do anything but continue, like a snake in a bamboo tube. I often don't understand the processes I go through; I can't feel the edges or limits of engagement. But I'm learning to feel safe relaxing into each moment, giving myself over to whatever comes.

The difference for me began when I found my own teacher. I'd been looking over the Tibetan Rinpoches who visited Dorje Ling the way they used to look at the horses back in Kentucky. I kept hoping for a connection, a clap of thunder, a bolt of lightning, a sign. I'd hoped I'd find a teacher but was afraid that I wouldn't. Hope and fear, they say, are big obstacles on the path. Hope and fear have to go. I had the notion, the concept, that my teacher would be one of the big Rinpoches from Asia, but it turned out that he had been standing next to me for years. A Western senior student who had been made a lama. None other than Lama P. himself.

It happened like this. When I decided to take a real (meaning I didn't have to cook) retreat with Lama P. up in Oregon, I began to have dreams in which he gave me instructions, advice, telling me how my mind worked, what to do when I fixated, why I was having so much trouble on the cushion. Ways to correct this. His advice worked. Then I began to talk to him in person when he had interviews with all of us on retreat. We'd been friends since I first came to Dorje Ling, so there was none of the terror that struck me tongue-tied with the Tibetan masters. Or the embarrassment that came when I'd suddenly start sobbing so deeply that I couldn't talk. But in Lama P. I felt a lightness, a willingness to help if that was needed, and a willingness to let me be and work it out on my own.

I remembered a dream I'd had soon after I came to Dorje Ling. I had to get to the top of a very complicated, multileveled house with labyrinthine passages and connecting tunnels. "I can't do this," I said in the dream, looking around hopelessly. Then Lama P. took my elbow, lightly as an angel. "I'll show you. Not that hard."

I'd forgotten this dream until I went on retreat with him. Since those weeks in Oregon, things have started to shift for me, to open. I couldn't perceive the extent of the changes in myself until the visits to my family. Where ice had been, now there was flow. I used to long for the day when I'd be cooked, but now I'm just grateful that I've found my way into this particular pot, happy that the cooking continues. I thank my teachers for their blessings and the *sangha* for their examples. I thank all of the kitchens I have ever worked in, even though I didn't know at the time that they were steps on my path.

May my experiences be of benefit to others.